Gently Down the Stream

By the same author:

Revelry by Night
Land of Promise

Gently Down the Stream

Notes from an Endangered Species

by J. Lawrence Barnard

WALKER AND COMPANY
NEW YORK

First published in the United States of America in 1976 by the Walker Publishing Company, Inc.

Published simultaneously in Canada by Fitzhenry & Whiteside, Limited, Toronto

ISBN: 0-8027-0552-9

Library of Congress Catalog Card Number: 76-16314

Printed in the United States of America

Book design by Robert Barto

10 9 8 7 6 5 4 3 2 1

Sept 8, 1992

To
D.K.B.

ACKNOWLEDGMENTS

In addition to thanking all the people who have made me laugh and the few who have made me think, I would like to acknowledge the typing of my manuscript by Ann Moore, the enthusiasm and understanding of both Wilson Gathings, my editor, and Sam Walker, my publisher—and above all the efforts of Barbara Kerr, who has nurtured this book since it was no more than a gleam in the author's eye.

J.L.B.

A man said to the universe:
"Sir, I exist!"
"However," replied the universe,
"The fact has not created in me
A sense of obligation."

—Stephen Crane

CHAPTER

Radakrishna, the majordomo of my rented houseboat on the Dal Lake in Kashmir, was a Brahmin. Although in appearance he looked like one of those roly-poly turbaned eunuchs in a *Playboy* cartoon, he was a highly educated man wedded to philosophic discussion. One hazy afternoon he joined me on the verandah to watch the sunset over the Himalayas. The dim block of the mountains changed from gray to purple. I was a young man then and we talked about nirvana. "This time," said Radakrishna, "I hope to achieve it." He murmured something in Hindi, rolling back his eyes until only the whites were showing. Suddenly, his eyes came down out of his head and he looked at me intently. "You may too," he said. The thought shook me. I'm not one for losing myself in the greater whole. "In your past lives," he continued, "you earned merit, because your present life is a favored one. You should escape reincarnation." I started to ask what would happen if this time around I blotted my copybook, then thought better of it. I knew he would have me back in the next as a sweeper, or maybe a toad.

Looking back over the years, I think he was right about my life being favored. I can't say that I ever accomplished much in my prime, but as James Michener says, a man can consider himself a success if he manages during his life to stay out of jail or a mental institution. This I have done to date. On the more positive side, I have been married thirty-six years—one year longer than the span of Mozart's lifetime—and although from time to time, my wife and I have struck discordant notes, on the whole our music has been good. We share the same inept approach to the world and laugh at the same things. We have three married daughters. They look upon me as a harmless crackpot, but also consider me one of the sources of their own peculiarities to which they are deeply attached. My sons-in-law are successful, two bankers and a lawyer. The bankers enrich my life by enjoying with me the pleasures of drink, backgammon, shooting and sailing; the lawyer by being a walking encyclopedia and literary man as well as an amateur woodsman. Their offspring, naturally, are all potential geniuses. I am also blessed with two dogs and two cats, four exceptional animals of low degree, three of whom sleep on our bed. I live in the country and have a boat, a thirty-eight-foot ketch, on which I often just sit in the harbor. My wife views the boat as a needless expense and says I would be equally happy in a treehouse. Luckily, because I never would have made it myself, I have inherited a little money —no vast sum to be sure, in any revolutionary debacle I would be in the next to last tumbril, but enough to support a boat. If you add to this advantage the fact that I am a WASP (White Anglo-Saxon Protestant), went to the "right" schools, belong to the "right" clubs, and live on the Eastern seaboard, any number of people will throw up their hands in horror.

In defense of WASPs in general, I can only say that there are many different types. When we are good, we are very, very good—big on integrity, independence, and intelligence —and when we are bad we're not horrid, just sanctimonious—a caste that clings to the status quo ante-bellum when our crowd was dominant in the country. Offensive perhaps, but a very low-key minority. I am somewhere in between these types, leaning more, I hope, towards the former than the latter. Some might call me a snob because I keep the Social Register in the bathroom, but it is only there as backup reading matter along with Scott's *U.S. Postage Stamp Catalogue* (1949), *An Atlas of the Stars*, and Liebetrau's *Oriental Rugs*. I admit to enjoying old houses, clubs and "reading rooms" with their nostalgic aura of sporting prints and panelled walls, flock wallpaper, lighted portraits of anybody's distinguished forbears, leather-bound sets of books regardless of their contents and Uncle Aymar's Netsuke collection. These faded trappings of privilege are music to my soul.

Before anyone throws up on my WASPish gabardine, I am not writing a polemic in favor of this isolated sect. I also belong to a far larger group, i.e., life's underachievers. Most of us, given a lever, are more likely to trip over it than move the world. This book is for those who have never met a payroll and may not even be on one. How can one enjoy life in the process of underachieving? To get around any latent feeling of inadequacy, I suggest philosophic perspective. Robert Ardrey says of mankind that we are a species six feet high and seventy years long, with delusions of grandeur about our creation. If we buy his concept, and I do, it's a great leveller. While some may have better seats than others, and some may grab them, we are all stumble-bums headed together for a destination of no one's choosing. Pessimistic? Perhaps. But we can make it a constructive pessimism since under the circumstances no one should take himself too seriously. Some time ago in troublous times (about the turn of the century) the City Library in Springfield, Mass. published a list of some of its available titles under the heading "Cheerful Books." I like to think that this autobiography would have been on the list. I have charted herein the petty accidents of fortune that have afflicted me, the innocent, in the pursuit of happiness. Although in the course of living, the heady wine of success has been meted out in thimbles, this niggardliness on the part of the wine steward has in no way impaired the meal. The simple reason is written in the Book of Proverbs —"He that is of merry heart hath a continual feast."

As far as I know, I first appeared in this world nine months to the day after my parents were married. For what in my life was a momentous occasion, the two principals involved seemed to show a shocking lack of concern. Father was shooting in Canada and Mother nearly had me in a box at the Metropolitan Opera during a performance of *Tristan*. It so happens that I am extremely fond of Wagner, but this can be attributed less to prenatal influence than to the fact that Mother used to scratch my back at bedtime and tell me stories of *The Ring*. This early grounding was later reinforced at a silent film on Africa when the pianist in the orchestra pit, accompanying a charge of elephants, played "The Ride of the Valkyries." My first recollections are not of the haunting French horn but of a squeaky phonograph record that featured a musical dialogue between a Mr. Gallagher and a Mr. Shean. Father had bought for the nursery a Victor talking machine with a large trumpet attached, just like in the advertisement of the dog listening to "His Master's Voice." I played it incessantly, alternating Messrs. Gallagher and Shean with "The March of the Wooden Soldiers," our only other selection. It was a happy time with only one small cloud on the horizon. In that zipperless era, my leather leggings were a definite burden. When my nurse buttoned me up in them, she used a button hook that invariably pinched when she got above the knee. I realized then that into each life a little rain must fall. Over the years, many people have told me that suffering is somehow meaningful but, looking back, this legging experience seems at just about the right level to keep it.

With Nunny

My Irish nurse, Nunny (*not* Nanny), and I had a delightful relationship. When I was in my leggings, looking rather chic for my age, she was also buttoned up to the throat in a well-cut dark blue overcoat, topped by a Mary Poppins cap held on by a white ribbon. Together we would set forth from our brownstone stoop at 105 East 65th Street for Central Park, where she would sit on a bench with the other nurses. At the Museum of Natural History in New York, there used to be a diorama showing an Eskimo fishing. Hunched in his furs over a hole in the ice into which his line disappeared, he had two fish laid out on the ice beside him. I used to emulate him in the Park, hunched contentedly over a frozen puddle in which I had cut a hole and dropped a piece of string. Sometimes we would proceed down Park Avenue with me on roller skates. One of the great blocks for roller skating was the west side of Park Avenue between 64th and 65th Streets, where there were several grocery stores and a fish store, Wynne and Trainor. A corrugated tin roof jutted out from the stores to stanchions at the curb, and the sidewalk was made up of great square blocks of slab. The moment you hit this block, your skates became inaudible and you glided over the surface as if on oil. Farther down, opposite St. Bartholomew's, there were a series of little hourglass parks in the middle of the avenue that Nunny used to favor because of their benches, but the paving was brick, scratchy and noisy, and the skating hopeless. I used to sit on the bench beside her listening to tales of the "ould country" that she told with fervor and much laughter. Somehow I felt she was always glad to be here.

On Tuesdays and Fridays, when I was older, we would bundle up and ride on the top of the Fifth Avenue bus for air, on the way to report for duty with the Knickerbocker Greys in the Seventh Regiment Armory. These bus rides, in full regimentals, were always embarrassing to me. The privates in the Greys at that time had to wear the round pillbox hats of bellhops, and this item of the uniform galled my infant ego. The officers all had proper hats with visor and plume—blue and white for a lieutenant, all blue for a captain, white for a major, red and white for a lieutenant colonel and a glorious full red for the colonel.

In my day, this little band of potential fascists (the term had not been invented) raggedly marched around the armory led by a slovenly retired captain in an olive-drab army cloak who tootled martial airs on a cornet. I rose through the ranks to lieutenant, primarily because Father was captain of Company K in the Seventh, which was the parent organization. The acquisition of a sword in addition to the plumed hat went straight to my head. Despite Father's position, I was almost immediately broken back to the ranks for fencing in the washroom and ripping the tunic off one of my fellow officers. This disciplinary action was probably all to the good of the corps since, in my brief period of glory, I had already marched my company into a wall, having panicked and forgotten to shout "squads right." I was beginning to realize that I was not an organization man.

Bovée School, which I attended, was a small, expensive school for boys run by two maiden ladies in a remodeled private house at 65th Street and Fifth Avenue. The Misses Eleanor and Kate Bovée were the counterparts of Miss Doasyouwouldbedoneby and Miss Bedonebyasyoudid in *The Water Babies.* Eleanor was a gentle dreamy soul, but Kate was ferocity itself. In retrospect, her disciplinary method seems peculiarly savage: She pulled hair. An offender would be seized by the topknot and dragged screaming out of the room. Mr. Lockman, the Latin teacher, was also a hairpuller, but his grip was never as firm as Miss Kate's. Among my classmates so victimized were a few who went on to better things—Douglas Fairbanks Jr., the

Topping brothers and Huntington Hartford. There was also a pudgy little boy called Duveen, of the Duveen galleries, who was a particular object of Mr. Lockman's rage, and a Sedgwick from Boston who was very pale and very bright.

A football team would be mustered in the afternoons. We would sally forth in our beautiful Abercrombie and Fitch uniforms to play in Central Park. Occasionally we played a pickup team of West-side toughs, swift Assyrian types in sneakers and cast-off, padded headgear such as you see in early photographs. When they saw us coming in our new domed helmets, a shout went up of pure sadistic joy. Needless to say, we were pulverized.

Summer life was less brutal. Each spring the house on 65th Street would be put to bed in the most elaborate fashion. Rugs were rolled up and wrapped in brown paper, white dust sheets were placed on everything, including the moose head in the dining room. It was a happy time with great promise in the air, along with the smell of camphor. When moving day came, the cook, the waitress, two chambermaids, and the luggage were driven twenty miles to Lawrence, Long Island in the morning. Harold, the chauffeur, returned in the afternoon for Mother, Nunny and me. Father escaped all this by taking the train.

The house in Lawrence was a Stanford White beach cottage of brown shingle with a *porte cochère* and a long porch that went halfway around it embedded in blue hydrangeas. It was situated off a sandy lane behind a tall privet hedge. Bannister Lane started at the Newbold Lawrence house and ran out in the marsh to a small dock where I used to go crabbing with Harold. Pink and blue mallows, the smell of bayberry and the sound of the sea on the outer sand bar were among my earliest sensations. Also mosquitoes. Although every window and door in the house was heavily screened, the ceiling of my room at night was an entomologist's delight. Before the days of Flit, the approved

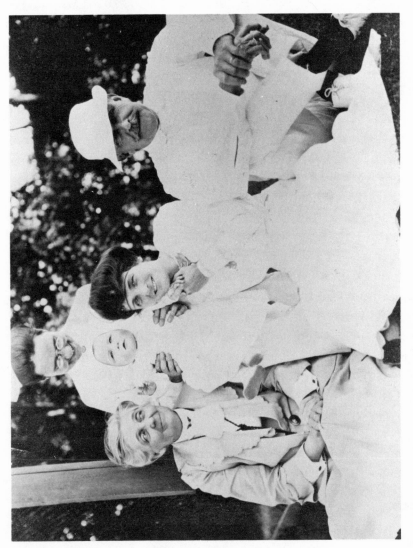

Doting relations on Bannister Lane

method for dealing with mosquitoes was primitive in the extreme. Mother or Nunny would steal into my room in response to my piteous moans, armed with long sticks at the end of which were shallow round pans filled with kerosene. Gingerly so as not to spill, the pan would be raised to the ceiling and in theory the mosquitoes would drop into it. The moment the pan started upward, the mosquitoes would take off unless they were asleep.

Although by no means imposing in its day, this "beach cottage" would be considered highly impractical by modern standards, with its five maid's rooms on the third floor and hot-air heat throughout. On chilly days in the fall before we went back to town, I remember the ladies in their long skirts were very partial to the grilled vents in the floor. The decor was pure Father, which at its best was sort of an imitation Scottish baronial and at its worst incorporated such items as a grandfather's clock and radio combination. The clock was put out by the Crosley Radio Company, of which he was a director. It was tall and skinny with a shiny walnut veneer and a hidden speaker where the chimes should have been. Much to Mother's distress this object stood for years in a corner of the living room, competing for her disfavor with the stuffed heads of elk, caribou, and stag that adorned the walls.

Every night at seven during Roosevelt's first term, Father would turn on the radio and listen to Fulton Lewis berating F.D.R. Mother used to ask Father why, if things were as bad as he and Mr. Lewis thought, the President had not been impeached. Father, who would have loved this, had long since dismissed the thought as impractical. Her question never failed to annoy him, which, unfortunately, was why she asked it. She approved highly of Eleanor Roosevelt. To describe Father as a black Republican would be to understate the case. He was brought up in the Horatio Alger tradition and any thought of sharing the wealth was anathema to him. This is not to say he was blind to the needs of the poor. He just firmly believed that if government gave the green light to business everything would take care of itself.

He was also something of a martinet. It came from all that marching and stamping around in unison that went on in the Seventh Regiment Armory. The Seventh prided itself on being as good if not better than West Point in its drill routine. As a captain, Father would bark out an order and his men would react smartly and with precision. It never worked that way at home.

Occasionally, Mother and I would be dragooned under his command for some task about the place. Too often this took the form of spraying the trees for aphids. The trees looked fine to us, and the gardener said there were no aphids, but there was no stopping Father once he got the bit in his teeth. The spraying machine was a clumsy contrivance consisting of an enormous barrel on wheels in which there was a pump attached to a hose, which in turn was attached to a ten-foot pole with a nozzle on the end. Mother and I, like a pair of Chinese coolies, would pull the wretched barrel into position. This was not easy, as it was heavy as lead when full. As we approached the chosen tree, Father would bark instructions:

"More to the east . . . No! East!"

"I do wish your Father would use right and left instead of the points of the compass," Mother would say sadly.

"I think he means left," I would answer.

Once in position, Father would squirt the trees with the pole, while Mother and I took turns pumping. He never could understand why we didn't enjoy this quite as much as he did.

The members of the staff at this time were all characters. Frank Smith, the gardener, looked as if he had just stepped off the cover of the *Saturday Evening Post*, complete with blue denim trousers, held up by suspenders, and a straw hat. He had never been to New York City, although he had lived all his life only twenty miles away. Long Island was good enough for his father and it was good enough for him. He once ventured as far as Far Rockaway.

Delia, the cook, on the other hand, was a displaced person in the country. She was a deeply religious Roman Catholic whose life in town revolved around the Church of St. Vincent Ferrer on Lexington Avenue. A plump, white-haired, motherly soul, when not turning out excellent meals, she was on her knees praying for remission of God knows what sins. Her demise was poetic, sudden, and just what she would have wanted. She was hit by a taxi on Lexington Avenue and died on the steps of St. Vincent Ferrer.

Marg began as a chambermaid, but as I grew up and Nunny moved on to other fields, Marg inherited me. She was the absolute spirit of devotion—so much so that when in later life I would come home tipsy from a debutante party and throw up out of the bedroom window, she would get a ladder in the early morning and wash it off the side of the house so Father wouldn't know. It's the kind of thing a man looks for all his life and seldom finds. Unfortunately Marg herself took to drink as the years progressed and Mother eventually had to fire her. I was away at college at the time, but it has always seemed to me that the life of a devoted Irish maid, bound by the strictest Catholicism, has all the makings of a drama worthy of O'Neill.

There was another maid called Bridget who stole my wife's engagement ring and ten years later gave it back. Can you imagine the agonies in the confessional? Harold, the chauffeur, was even lazier than I, so we had a strong bond in common. Driving in and out of the city, I would sit on his lap and steer. Harold taught me what can only be described as "creative driving"—that gentle sliding from lane to lane with a touch of speed to pass. I've been indebted to him all my life, although other members of my family do not share my enthusiasm. In this little group I enjoyed an early stardom, yacketing away in the maid's dining room over a cup of cambric tea, or watching the sun sink in the marshes from the maid's porch at the back of the house.

Although we moved out somewhat earlier, summer always seemed to start with the Fourth of July. At the crack of dawn I would be out in the lane on my bicycle with cap pistols, bombs, and firecrackers bought in the neighboring Italian town of Inwood. After breakfast Father, Mother and I, in our Sunday-best, would pile into what Father insisted on calling the "shooting-brake"—actually the first station wagon put out by the Dodge Brothers—and drive to the Beach Club's ferry landing.

Three covered launches in various stages of disrepair carried the local gentry across the inlet to the outer sandbar, now named Atlantic Beach. The pride of the fleet was the *Agnes*, a solid tub of a boat that held about thirty people. After an endless walk through the dunes on a boardwalk (which grew shorter as one grew up) the beach on the ocean side was finally reached—and the shingled shed where Jim, the manager, and his German wife presided over root beer and chocolate oreo sandwiches. Fanning out from their emporium were several rows of wooden bathhouses.

Jim's forbears must have been Indian chiefs. Tall, with a splendid physique, and a noble, bronzed face, he was manager, lifeguard, swimming teacher, and a friend of everyone, yet possessed of a quiet reserve that bred enormous respect. On the Fourth of July he would dress up as Uncle Sam, complete with goatee, striped red and white trousers, a blue silk frock coat and a Lincolnesque top hat —a truly magnificent figure leading the parade of parasoled mothers and white-flanneled fathers up and down the beach to the patriotic strains of the village band. In later years when the club grew grander and acquired a swimming pool and a proper restaurant, Jim still appeared—from where no one knew—to perform his traditional role.

Sailing was a big summer feature. I was given a small sailboat known as a sneak-box, which I raced every Wednesday and Saturday up and down the inlet. Sundays, the children raced in the ocean with the grown-ups in the slightly larger, one-design class called Raters, gaff-rigged with marvelous overhanging sterns. With such constant exposure to the sport, I should have gotten better at it; yet almost every week I would upset and have to be fished out of the sea by one or the other of two older, very neat, bluff and hearty seafaring cousins who monitored the races from their fishing craft. The mounting scorn for their inept relative as the season progressed was sometimes hard to take as their resonant voices boomed over the water. Their scorn was nothing, however, compared to my father's when at his command I threw over the anchor one day and watched in frozen fascination as line *and* anchor disappeared in the deep.

The Sunday races were adult, and typical of those up and down the Eastern seaboard. First there was the ritual on the lawn at home of putting up the spinnaker in stops. The boats would be towed out of Rockaway Inlet, (there was no Atlantic Beach bridge at the time) and we would race a triangular course usually involving Ambrose Channel lightship as one of the markers. On our return to the Cedarhurst Yacht Club, then, as now, a remodeled houseboat on top of a barge, there would be an enormous tea with cocoanut and chocolate layer cakes.

Bicycle polo was another favored sport. The grown-ups thought very highly of it as training for the real thing. Once they even lent us the club field which was foreshortened for the occasion, but the surface was turf and the pedalling was too difficult. We had all the trimmings though—extra mallets (sawed-off big ones) laid out on polo coats and barley water between the periods, even a few ladies on the verandah.

One should never underestimate the importance of the latter to a game of polo. When the club sold off some land to avoid taxes, the polo field was moved away from the club house, but with no verandah and no ladies the game went the way of the dodo. I had a pony called China who was blind in one eye and needed about three men to hold him down while I mounted. Once up, for some reason, he was docile as a lamb. In front of the club house this little exhibition of equestrian skill would cause an occasional murmur of appreciation among the ladies, but on the new field, minus the verandah and ladies, it was like the sound of one hand clapping in the wilderness or whatever it is Zen Buddhists enjoy.

Although Mother maintained that she hated the life in Lawrence and much preferred New York City, the former was the heart and core of her life. Very family oriented, Mother knew virtually no one who was not a Lawrence in one form or another. Not to be confused with the Boston Lawrences and their Bishop, the New York Lawrences were an equally venerable lot. William Lawrence, the founding father, came over from England in 1635 on the good ship *Planter*. According to my Great-aunt Carrie, who went in for genealogy when not working out on parallel bars in her attic, William was descended from Sir Robert Lawrence, one of Richard Coeur de Lion's barons and the first to mount the ramparts at the siege of Acre. William married Elizabeth Smith, daughter of the founder of Smithtown, Long Island. Whether Elizabeth was impressed by his illustrious heritage is unrecorded, but it seems more likely she enjoyed his being a patentee of Flushing and the largest landed proprietor therein (Shea Stadium, World's Fair Grounds, etc.). Elizabeth was big on land. She eventually married Sir Philip Carteret who had just inherited New Jersey.

Sir Osbert Sitwell maintains that ancestors stretch out behind one like the tail of a peacock. Mother never strutted, being a most shy and retiring soul, but she was eminently secure in this field. Father used to twit her about her royal blood. In this same flight of seventeenth-century forebears appearing on these shores there was another called William Tangier Smith (no relation to Elizabeth). At the tender age of sixteen, William, whose mother was an English lady-in-waiting to the Queen of Portugal, was appointed Governor of Tangier in Africa. The Portuguese at the time had great plans for the development of Tangier and I can only conclude that the King, in handing out this plum to her son, must have had something going with his wife's lady-in-waiting sixteen years before. The Tangier project apparently failed and William hastened to the New World where he seemed to have prospered. He became Colonel William Tangier Smith, chief justice of the Province of New York and the owner of the Manor of St. George in Suffolk County, Long Island. The Manor, part of which is now Setauket, originally included forty miles of beach that brought in a sizable income from whales washed up on the shore. A contemporary of the colonel describes him as follows: "The finest silks and lace covered his judicial person . . . When he walked, a silver-headed cane supported him and he rode on a fancy velvet saddle . . . occasionally he affected a Turkish scimitar."

In contrast to these well-heeled Long Island people, Father's forebears were more pedestrian. "My father came of an exceedingly long line of ascertained persons, all entirely undistinguished," wrote E. F. Benson of his forebears. The same dictum applies to mine. In a laudable attempt to establish some relationship with Barnard Castle in Durham, England, Father wound up in the clutches of the College of

Heralds in London which, for a fee, will trace one's family back to the Doomsday Book. Father drew the line at one Richard Barnard (1522-1591) ten generations back, because he was getting further and further away from Barnard Castle and bogging down in a mess of minor squires in the depths of Essex.

Richard was armigerous, but aside from having a coat of arms and a small manor named Lashley Hall, his chief distinction was that he left a sum of money in his will to the poor of Stebbing Parish. (The amount is indecipherable.) His son, John Barnard, married Joan Lindsell of Lindsell, Essex, and produced a hardy offspring called Bartholomew. At the advanced age of sixty-one, the latter decided he wanted no part of England's domestic difficulties. The country was hopelessly divided; Charles I was preparing for war with Scotland; Cromwell had not yet appeared on the scene but Parliamentary Party mobs were rioting in London. So in 1639 he left for America with his son, who had just come of age.

After landing in Boston, Bartholomew's initial mistake was a bad one—he turned right instead of left and headed for Maine. Far from repairing the family fortunes, he was apparently driven to trade (carpentry, I believe). After eight years of freezing and building log cabins with his father, Bartholomew Jr. established himself as a landowner a little further south. In 1647 he joined the newly formed Hartford colony, which had been organized in the rich valley of the Connecticut River. According to the New England historian Norman Isham, the Hartford colonists were "quiet, steady people" who soon "pushed their boundaries before them into the wilderness and gave evidence that they were to be the dominating element in the new territory."

Bartholomew Jr. flourished in this environment until he died at the age of eighty in 1698. His son, John Barnard, sergeant-at-law, was something of a misfit among the quiet, steady people. The only other person I ever heard of with the rather dubious title of sergeant-at-law was Sergeant Buzfuz in *The Pickwick Papers*, who prosecuted Mr. Pickwick for having designs on his landlady. Although the title indicates one of a superior order of barristers, my predecessor's one recorded courtroom appearance fails to show him at his best. The Hartford County Records, 4 September 1705, contains the following notation:

"Elizabeth Church of Hartford, a single woman . . . breach of law by committing fornication . . . appeared and confessed the fact. (She is fined 50 shillings.) John Barnard appeared . . . he did not account himself as the father of the child . . . This court do adjudge the said John Barnard to be the father of the said child, begotten of the said Elizabeth. (He is to pay 2s 6d per week for the maintenance of the child for four years after birth of same.)"

Although the maintenance charges for the child cannot be called excessive by modern standards, there is a lesson in all this for the would-be Connecticut fornicator. The Court stated that the reason for finding John Barnard the father of the child was that, according to the midwife's testimony, Elizabeth in travail repeatedly accused him and no other. The Connecticut law, originally passed in 1692, requires that the mother be "constant in the charge in travail"—and this is the state law today.

The little two-shillings-sixpence chap grew up in time to sire a child of his own, another John Barnard but a worthier eye in my peacock's tail than his grandfather of the same name. This John Barnard was a soldier, Captain of the Third Connecticut Regiment, which fought under Lafayette and won the praise of Washington at Yorktown. Earlier, as a junior officer in 1756, he attests to the glory of the English forces of the period in his laconic diary of the Crown Point expedition against the French on Lake Champlain.

"Sunday the 29th—Very rainy day, cold storm. Four men whipped.

"Monday the 30th—At night we had an alarm and a man was killed in the fort by one of our own men. He was shot through the private parts.

"Tuesday the 31st—Cleared off very pleasant. Sundry men whipped. Nothing remarkable.

"Wednesday, the 1st—Heard that a Highlander killed a Stockbridge Indian at Fort Edward. The Indian fired upon him and did not kill him. The Highlander took after him, shot him and cut off his head. He took out his heart and brought it in.

"Thursday—This day I got King's Stores—nine ounces of pork and a pound of bread and a half pound of pees and our men would take none of it and made a great noise and cried 'home, home, home, no meat'."

Apparently my forebear had thoughts of home himself. Although the French and Indian War dragged on for another seven years, he showed up the following year in Hartford, married to a lady named Hannah Bigelow. He also bought a house from her father (of which more later).

Somewhat arbitrarily I think, Osbert Sitwell fixes the point at which our forebears become ancestors at the great-great-grandparent generation. (Sixteen in all.) Fourteen of my lot were white Anglo-Saxon Protestants; one was an Italian and one was a Dane. The WASPs on the whole appear to have been well enough off, but there was not an eye on the peacock's tail among them. The Dane and the Italian, however, add a little luster. John Balthazar Uytendael, Baron von Bretton, was a big plantation owner in St. Croix, Virgin Islands. According to my grandmother, one day a young Italian seafarer named Augustus Zerega (her father) arrived at the Baron's door. Augustus had left his native town of Zerega, north of Genoa, with nothing but an astrolabe; matrimonially, he appeared as no great catch. However, when the door opened Augustus found himself in the hall with the Baron's daughter—a little girl of thirteen—sliding down the bannisters. Apparently, she slid right into his arms and they were married and lived happily ever after. Strangely enough, the *mise en scène* of their marital bliss was in the Bronx. Augustus parlayed his astrolabe into a small merchant fleet that plied the China trade and built a place on Long Island Sound called Island Hall. The last shore-based pylon of the Whitestone Bridge now stands on the site, and the only memorial to their idyll is a large green signpost on Bruckner Boulevard with the inscription "Zerega Avenue."

It seems inevitable that proximity to the city constitutes a death warrant for any house that once supplied what is now known as gracious living. Another great-grandfather, Newbold Lawrence, grew up on his father's country place on the Hudson. The house, a handsome example of Greek Revival architecture, used to stand on what is now the corner of 133rd Street and Riverside Drive. On the death of his father, John Burling Lawrence, the property was sold and Newbold moved to Long Island, where he purchased a large tract of land near Far Rockaway. The nearest railroad station at the time was Jamaica, ten miles away. Through his efforts the railway was extended from Jamaica to the coast and over the years the land was developed into the suburban areas of Lawrence and Cedarhurst. A house-party, described by my great-aunt Carrie in 1877, gives an account of beach picnics, crabbing, sailing on the inlet, and Fourth of July fireworks. It was a gentler era than our own, and certainly less populous. Atlantic Beach, now a metropolis, was then a deserted sandbar, and inshore the Rockaway Hunt hallooed over wide open fields that now are parking lots and houses all in a row.

I never knew either of my grandfathers. One married a daughter of the aforesaid Newbold Lawrence and the other a daughter of Augustus Zerega of Bruckner Boulevard fame. All I know about the former is that he enjoyed doing the offbeat and once spent a summer travelling through Spain in a donkey cart. He also used to rub champagne into his scalp which he maintained accounted for his snowy white hair beloved by all the ladies. My other grandfather was a Yale graduate and ostensibly a lawyer, but he was more interested in reading French plays than in carving out a career in corporate law. Unfortunately, this esoteric interest in Gallic drama coincided with his father-in-law's obstinate view that steam would never triumph over sail. The results were disastrous financially. While the United States was burgeoning in all directions and the Astors, Vanderbilts, Harrimans, and others were coming up in the world, grandfather and his father-in-law, on whom he rather depended, found themselves well on the way in the opposite direction. The family carried on in reduced circumstances, which in those days meant only a cook and a maid, no coachman, at 38 East 35th Street in New York City.

Presiding over this ménage in which my father grew up was his mother, an indomitable little woman who lived to be ninety-five and whose lifetime spanned twenty-four presidencies from Martin Van Buren to Franklin Roosevelt. Following the death of her husband, she always wore widow's weeds and a starched white crinoline cap with ribbons that made her look like Queen Victoria. I used to be taken to have tea with her. The tea was known as Mr. Morgan's tea and we drank it out of beautiful cups, Crown Derby, I imagine, while waiting for father who paid her a daily visit on his way home from Wall Street. She was then living in an apartment house on Park Avenue below Grand Central Station in the area known as Murray Hill. I can still see the living room with its long red velvet curtains, the dark portrait of her grandfather, the Danish baron, glowering down at me, and all available wall space a jumble of gold-framed water colors of the Nile, camels, pyramids, Amalfi, and the Italian lakes; also two ormolu display cabinets, in one a collection of demitasse spoons, in the other a collection of thimbles. Despite her age, she played a sharp game of backgammon, which I like to think she taught me.

My mother and grandmother never got on. They were poles apart in temperament, and the fact that they shared Father between them didn't make matters any easier. Mother, as I have said, was very family oriented, *her* family that is. The only exception among her intimates was another family clan named Williams, who also lived on the same lane in Lawrence and whose titular head was a distinguished and highly polished mahogany tycoon. There were two sisters the same age as Mother and several brothers who looked upon her as a wild, black-haired belle. Under Mr. Williams' aegis the three girls went to Egypt one winter with a courier called Snug; life for her then was at its apogee. It's sad to contemplate, but everybody's life does have an apogee.

Father entered this tightly-knit group all fired up with plans for becoming a tycoon himself. Island Hall, the Zerega place on the Sound, had been sold in the face of the relentless triumph of steam, and as his own father's law practice had never produced any money, he had to start from scratch. The money appeared again through his abilities on Wall Street, which were followed with keen interest by grandmother for whom he had always been a boy wonder. Mother knew nothing about money and cared less. She considered talk of money to be "common." They had never talked about it at home. After a whirlwind courtship their life together began to wilt on the vine. In addition to being interested in making money, Father was a sailing man and an excellent shot. Mother's outdoor life was limited to walking and a little lawn tennis, which she played very well using an underhand serve. But the problem lay deeper than different tastes. I discovered this much later when looking at the family chart. Jammed up in the top of the box for my generation was my name with plenty of space underneath for at least a dozen brothers and sisters. But there were no more names. Father, I gather, solaced himself elsewhere, and Mother, through ignorance or lack of interest, did nothing to cope.

I filled a gap in her life for a while. We did a lot of people-watching together, happily sitting in the lobbies of European hotels while Father was shooting in Scotland. But after several summers of this I began to realize that Mother was sacrificing herself (and me) on the altar of good taste. Taste was the one yardstick by which she judged mankind. We once saw a Mickey Mouse film to which mother took violent exception. I forget what poor Mickey did, but he became her *bête noir* and symbolized all she disliked about the present. Brought up in the sheltered days when there was a furnaceman and a clockman to wind the clocks, she withdrew more and more into herself as the twentieth century progressed.

Out of these ingredients my early years were formed. I was certainly influenced by them, but in the case of specific parental influence the results were rarely as intended. Enraged over the subject of Mickey Mouse, I once threw a plate at Mother. I never turned off a light in the house, one of Father's pet economies. I used to be a big spender at the Rockaway Hunt Club charging orangeades for all my little friends. At the end of the month Father went over his chits; he would explode at seeing my signature and accuse me of being "sneaky." My attitude remained unregenerate; I knew he would get the chits and my culpability was an open book. Naturally I shrank from his tirades, but they didn't affect me at all. Outside factors are things to which something inside oneself may react, but the something remains unchanged. Maybe it's the "dweller within the body" as the Bhagavad Gita says. Maybe it's the soul. Whatever it is you are stuck with it for life, for better or for worse. I'm not uptight about the situation. I have enjoyed this self completely. In an era when so many have to learn how to be their own best friend, we have had a good time together.

CHAPTER

According to the Anthological Society of New England, St. Paul's School, Concord, New Hampshire, is a church school dedicated to "the education of the Christian scholar and gentleman." In my day it was a little kingdom ruled over by Dr. Samuel S. Drury, a formidable man of the cloth.

"The Drip," as the irreverent sometimes referred to him, made valiant attempts to establish relationships with the student body; but as he walked around the grounds dressed in a black cloak and a porkpie hat and affably waving his cane, there was a marked tendency on the part of the Christian scholars to act like chaff before the wind. Allegedly shy and certainly withdrawn, he was an earnest man who represented all that the school stood for; in fact, in later life, it was hard for me to think of the school without him.

It is too bad, but I remember him less for the theological content of his sermons than for a certain worldliness that crept into them on occasion. He had one in particular in which, as if by some divine revelation, he heard the rattle of mortar and pestle. To the cognoscenti, this only meant one thing. Some poor wretch had been caught doing something unspeakable, and his father was providing a new building in order to see his son graduate.

I was never in the mortar-and-pestle class myself, which

was reserved for the very rich, but at one point Father was the recipient of an ominous note, which I quote in full, as it has a certain flavor and throws considerable light on the character of the Rector, and I am afraid to some extent on my own.

> *Dear Mr. Barnard,*
>   *I feel genuinely troubled about Lawrence's attitude toward Sixth Form responsibility. He knows from me how keenly I want him to have a purposeful and strong last year at the School, and I have taken special pains to encourage him. When, however, a boy has a dentist appointment in town, goes to town for that purpose, and visits the airport instead and then tells me that he has "forgotten" the dentist, I feel myself dealing with an undependable character.*
>   *Can we not encourage your boy, both of us, toward a more staunch attitude toward life. Otherwise he may do something so foolish as to exclude himself from a complete course at St. Paul's.*
>   *Believe me,*
>
> > *Faithfully yours,*
> > *S.S. Drury*

Imagine trying to explain away this one at home. Although I did graduate, the Rector I feel had me pretty well typed. Some people are staunch; others are not. From the very beginning, bad attitude exuded from my every pore. Not that I was against the school, I was disaffiliated, but not insurrectionary. Rules and regulations were all very well for others, but they had no bearing on me. I don't think the Rector understood this. Neither did Father.

In my Second Form year I was "talked to"—that is, grilled by the Sixth Form Council. Since I was a passable athlete in the Lower School, it is just possible that the Council thought I was worth the trouble of berating. Athletic ability is often considered a virtue. It was a grim business nonetheless. The culprit was ushered into a dark room with one spotlight concentrated on a wicker chair while the school heroes sat in a deep semicircle in the shadows, tearing him apart. I remember I was a few minutes late and had the misfortune to enter this charmed circle with one of my shoelaces untied. Such a hullabaloo was made of this— indicative of my slipshod character—that I resolved then and there to think more of protective coloration in the future. In later years I have formulated from this early experience a maxim that I pass on to the slatternly—if you're going to be late, be neat.

The younger boys lived in dormitories—long, high-ceilinged rooms partitioned off into cubicles, about twenty down each side, with windows in the air space above the partitions. A cubicle was just large enough for a cot, a bureau, a small table, and a camp chair. This Spartan simplicity was usually alleviated by a red SPS blanket and a pillow from the college of one's choice. Privacy was furnished by a curtain at the open end. Four long, high radiators, covered with wooden slats for protection, occupied the center of the room. One of our chief delights of an evening, before "lights out," was to "roast" some unfortunate on the radiator. Roasting consisted of seizing the victim and holding him down on the wooden slats while comforters and blankets from all the cots were heaped on top of him. A favorite victim my year was a shy, retiring youth, probably something of a genius, who occasionally went berserk at the piano in the Common Room playing endless variations of "Who?"

In the process of manly development it is important to establish a name for yourself in some field of endeavor. Mine was eating shredded wheat. While others excelled on the playing fields or acquired scholastic honors, I had the distinction of eating twelve biscuits at one sitting. This was no small feat; they were bigger in those days, and there was a lot of cream and sugar involved.

One dish we were given—chipped beef in a creamy sauce

—was thought to contain saltpeter, a sexual depressant. We were assured that it didn't, but there was a definite credibility gap. Such stimulation as we had consisted of sneaking off to ogle the maid's dormitory, although the pulchritude therein was scarcely up to Minsky's. The stars were two young pudding-faced girls from Concord, one of whom was said to have been seduced by the goalie on the hockey team. My own exploit with the shredded wheat was pallid by comparison.

Father, of course, had given me the standard sex lecture at the end of the lane one summer—how bees take pollen and how men have one thing and women the opposite. He pointed out solemnly that putting the two together provided a very pleasurable sensation. I remember asking him if it was as good as back-scratching. He said better and we let it go at that. That afternoon we drove over to Roosevelt Raceway in Mineola where there was a big crowd gathered for a race. At least half the people there were opposites and the thought of them all with holes instead of penises had a certain passing fascination. I was rather young at the time.

At school, sexual education was not a part of the curriculum, but the school farm occasionally provided some sterling examples of sex in action. Word would get around that the bull was going to service some cows and a group of lascivious little urchins would trudge out to watch. My own sexual activity was confined to the climbing rope in the gymnasium. Although there was no friction involved, I soon discovered that the simple muscular effort of climbing hand over hand had a direct connection with my genitalia causing a paroxysm of pleasure on reaching the ceiling. As a result, in my Second Form year I developed quite formidable biceps. For the most part, quietly, we watched the ducks pecking and chasing each other on the School Pond. But all this was in the spring, and an idle thing at best.

In winter, the School Pond held five, sometimes six

hockey rinks separated from each other by solid board partitions about four feet high. A team of horses regularly shaved this ice, pulling behind them what looked like a wide rake, but which was really a knife. In those days there was virtually no skiing at school, maybe an oddball or two would fool around on Jerry Hill, but the fantastic upsurge of the sport didn't come until much later.

The brown sluice water that fed into the pond at the upper end from Little Turkey, from which our iced tea derived its name, looked almost black when it mingled with the main body of water in front of the chapel. The famous St. Paul's "black ice" hardened four or five feet thick and was crystal clear. The newly shaved surface of the ice had an almost oily slickness, black and glossy and very hard. To skate on this alone with a stick and a puck and to hear the latter crack against the sideboards was a sensation worthy of the gods. Night came early in winter and we used to skate until dark. At the end of the day we would crunch up on the packed snow in our skates to the "Tuck Shop" where you could buy milk and a marmalade sandwich—a touch of ambrosia for finale.

Winter was always very much with us in New Hampshire. As soon as you went outdoors after a shower, your hair immediately froze. In my Fifth Form year I lived in the now defunct Old Upper on a hill overlooking the Library Pond, and we had to walk around the pond a quarter of a mile to the New Upper to be fed. This became troublesome for tardy risers, of which the building was full, so my roommate and I, with the same acumen that made America great, bought a toboggan. The next morning we made a late run down the hill and across the pond to breakfast in about two minutes flat. The project was good but fairly short-lived—three or four days—as neither of us was particularly interested in hauling the toboggan back up the hill.

On Saturday nights in the winter months, members of

the Sixth Form had to give a speech to the whole school, assembled in what was then the "old school study." There were usually four or five speakers per night. Attendance, of course, was compulsory. Some people take to public speaking naturally, but I am not one of them. To say that most of my class were not gifted on their feet would be an understatement. The majority viewed the prospect with undisguised alarm, approaching dread. And there was no getting out of it. As my time to speak approached, I contracted "pinkeye" by rubbing toothpaste in my eyes and wearing dark glasses. The practice was much used in the spring because real "pinkeye" was extremely contagious and those who "got" it were confined to the "Infirmary" for two weeks. You couldn't study, so during the day you were free to commune with nature. The medicos soon caught on, however, owing to the faint smell of peppermint on the lids. My case was rejected out of hand.

Archie Cox, the Watergate prosecutor-to-be, preceded me on the podium and, I am sure, handled himself competently. I had no idea what he said as I was so shattered by the ordeal that I sat in a daze with sweaty palms repeating to myself my own memorized speech. My subject was Alexandre Dumas and to this day the opening line is engraved on my memory—"Grandson of a negress and son of one of Napoleon's generals, Alexandre Dumas was born in . . ." I got through it, but afterwards I was told nobody could hear it. Apparently, choked with fright, I had talked in a stage whisper. Another classmate whose subject was "Driving a 'tin Lizzie' across the United States" also failed to distinguish himself. Following a brave start with "I bought this secondhand car in New York City," he stopped dead, shuffled his feet, and rolled his eyes heavenwards during an agonizing pause which must have been a minute, but seemed like ten. Since it had become quite clear that the speaker's mind had gone blank, the Rector, who presided at these sessions, fixed him with a lionesque gaze and said, "You may step down now, Mr. Simpson." He had not even crossed the Hudson.

My last winter at school, a rather odd thing happened. Earlier in the fall the Rector had thundered from the pulpit that ten percent of the Sixth Form were rotten to the core and probably would be expelled if they didn't mend their ways. Actually he was right, we were a bad lot, but his subsequent actions were remarkable. The bad ten percent were gently garnered to his bosom. This took the form of our going to the rectory on Sunday evenings where he gave us Welsh rarebit and read passages from *Pilgrim's Progress*. An open fire was blazing in the hearth and, in addition to teaching us how to make a really good rarebit, the Rector in a black velvet smoking jacket showed us the distinctions between good and bad bookbinding with examples from his extensive library.

It was difficult because one never knew how much the Rector knew. I knew that one of our number had been off that same afternoon with one of the pudding-faced maids. Another had been gambling all day and had made a very good thing of it. My roommate and I had a car, an old Buick touring model hidden deep in the woods; others were smokers, which was then grounds for expulsion; and at least two overindulged in liquor. Had we known of pot and LSD, they certainly would have been represented.

And yet, there we were, being seduced by authority. It was ludicrous—but we *were* seduced. Although *Pilgrim's Progress* didn't accomplish much, not one of those bad actors got away scotfree from the civilizing impact of an open fire, Welsh rarebit, and Revere bindings in full Morocco leather. I still think of the tableau sometimes in my own library at home and the Warden gets full marks.

Chapel at school was a big thing. We had to go every morning and twice on Sundays. As it took some time for the whole school to file in and fill up the pews, many of those already seated could be seen bending over their Bibles during this period. Certainly, there is something in the good book for everyone. *Ecclesiastes* was a favorite with the sophisticated (there were a few in my class who started shaving in the Third Form and also read a new magazine called *The New Yorker*). The plain crass went in for the old prophets, particularly the twenty-third chapter of Ezekiel, a nice sexy passage about Aholah and Aholibah who had the teats of their virginity pressed by some lean young captains of horse.

Although my net godly intake from chapel was low on weekdays, the evening service on Sundays was quite a different affair. The staging was superb. The warm glow inside the chapel made a powerful contrast to the wintry blackness outside—candles flickered on the lectern, the back row stalls looked darker, and the stained glass windows a deep purple. The service ended with a prayer, which, out of all the claptrap, got through to me by its sheer beauty of expression. The Rector would read in his mellifluous voice, the congregation kneeling—"O Lord, support us all the day long, until the shadows lengthen and the evening comes, and the busy world is hushed, and the fever of life is over, and our work is done. Then in thy mercy grant us a safe lodging, and a holy rest, and peace at the last. Amen." I used to leave the chapel dazed by the comfort of it all.

Spring came to St. Paul's in little driblets—in tiny puddles, then big ones, and rivulets running through mud. Here and there in the thinning snow, croci appeared on the chapel lawn, forsythia buds began to sprout, and the great changeover gained momentum. Everybody felt it, even indoors in the gym where we sweated on the rowing machines in preparation for the eight-oared shells.

As the spring progressed, it became very hot, though the

water remained cold for a long time. There was one icy swimming place, an abandoned quarry quite high up in the hills where we used to drive in a hired buggy. Jogging along a single track lane through laurel, azaleas, and pink and white dogwood, the downhill side of the lane opened up in places and we looked out on America just as the first settlers saw it—nothing but trees as far as the eye could see. The thought of chopping a passage through them boggled the imagination. Had I lived in those days, there's no question about it, I would have been a river man myself.

Canoes were a big part of our life when the weather got warmer. Usually I lazed around in my canoe on the upper reaches of the School Pond watching the minutiae of nature working out their lives in the reeds. A big muskrat lived up there and had built a substantial house. One day I watched a duck with her three ducklings drifting around close to the muskrat's front door. I could see the muskrat swimming home and I thought it would be the end of a duckling, but the muskrat swam right past them into his house and the ducks didn't even look around. Nature, to a city boy, is a constant revelation. Sometimes I took a canoe trip from Little Turkey Pond, where every rock had a turtle or two dozing in the sun, then down a connecting stream through sedges to the sluice and back home to the School Pond. The last part of the trip was always the best. After a day of paddling in the sun, the sluice carried you effortlessly back in tree shade, somewhat faster than a Tunnel of Love.

We had one superb tradition known as "Cricket Holiday." This was a surprise holiday declared for no other reason than it was going to be a marvellous day which ought to be enjoyed. You could do with the day anything you wished, within the ground rules of the establishment. News came to us first at morning chapel when the Rector read a special lesson about "little children playing in the streets of Jerusalem." With these key words everybody knew at once that the day was theirs.

Going out for crew was the principal business of the spring term. The two rowing clubs, Halcyon and Shattuck, both put in the water seven or eight crews for eight-oared boats. The top crews rowed in shells, beautiful, long and sleek and light as feathers, whereas the lesser people rowed in what were called "barges," which were much less gainly and heavier, but did not upset so easily. I made it up the ladder to the shells but never to the first crew. This pained me, not because I was not in the top eight, but because I was vain and they were entitled to wear blazers with crossed oars on the pocket, red with white piping for Halcyon, and blue with white for Shattuck.

Each rowing day in the spring we would drive several miles up to Long Pond in horse-drawn wagons, also locally known as "barges." (One is currently in service at the Mystic Seaport.) The occupants sat facing each other and the neophytes, those who had been in the Lower School the preceding year, were rolled head over heels down the middle between two rows of knees as a form of initiation.

Two of these horse-drawn "barges," one Halcyon and one Shattuck, played a role at the graduation exercises. Part of the ceremonies took place at the flagpole on the green across from the chapel, and were attended by the Sixth Form, their families, and groups of "old boys" from reunion classes spanning more than fifty years. As the "barges" approached the flagpole, next year's captain of each rowing club stood on the box beside the driver, with his crew resplendent in blazers behind him. Long before they came into view, you could hear the crews singing in the distance, then the clip-clop of the horses' hooves. For the captains so honored, it must have been a high point in their lives. The oar of the captain of the winning crew was raised to the top of the flagpole while the band played "Auld Lang Syne."

Schmalz? Of course. St. Paul's, however, had a lot more to be said for it. In the 1920s the "Establishment" was still a tightly-knit going concern that had considerable financial and political power in the United States. Tradition was its cement. Schools like St. Paul's provided that cement. These schools instilled in the people who had that power, not only a common denominator of traditions such as those I've just cited, but also an aristocratic tradition in the best meaning of the word—a tradition of gentlemanly conduct. We were given a code of honor—one was a gentleman, and gentlemen always did the decent thing. Although this sounds fearfully British, it does have a lasting effect.

At the time I was more in the category of Evelyn Waugh's character, Captain Grimes. The captain was presented a bottle of whiskey and a loaded revolver, then left alone in a room with the expectation that he would do "the decent thing." At the end of twenty minutes, Grimes emerged happy as a grig, the whiskey bottle empty and the revolver still on the table. I've always sympathized with Captain Grimes. Nevertheless, the concept is a valid one in this day of changing values. My own version is that a gentleman is anyone who, for one reason or another, is above the struggle for personal advantage and, therefore, takes a gentle view of his fellow man.

St. Paul's standards were high (not that they preached *hara-kiri*), and they were considerably higher than mine. If there was a flaw in the system, it was that it produced too many who believed that God had made the status quo, although this attitude was a sign of the times. St. Paul's did its best to foster a sense of Christian altruism for the common good. Although the student body in my day was made up in large part of the grandsons of the same tough breed of nineteenth-century capitalists deplored by Henry Adams, the school tried to implant the idea that intelligent men of principle and foresight were needed in private enterprise and even in the government.

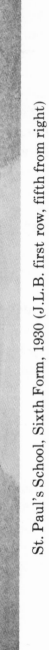

St. Paul's School, Sixth Form, 1930 (J.L.B. first row, fifth from right)

I didn't learn much at St. Paul's. I was a slow starter and the opinions expressed above came to me later, but as I grew up I began to realize that my school days there were both a privilege and an unforgettable experience. You don't have many of these in life.

The summer after school I was exposed to the Wild West on a dude ranch in Jackson Hole, Wyoming. Since I had never been further west before then than the Palisades Amusement Park on the far side of the Hudson, this opening up of the hinterland made a distinct impression. In the first place, it seemed to take forever to get there—those endless plains of wheat or whatever sliding by the train windows, then the badlands with their weirdo buttes. I found it all rather depressing and began to yearn for the neon lights of Broadway.

The ranch itself, when I finally got there, was somewhat better. Most of the people came from New York and I felt considerably less homesick. I was assigned an excellent cow pony, a lively pinto, and began to warm to my routine of riding into town in the morning to get the mail, a snooze after lunch, and bridge in the evening. From time to time we went on pack trips spending a night or two out on the range.

On one of these trips I had my first experience with a girl. Put that way it sounds rather dashing, which it certainly was not. The setting was near perfection—a warm clear night with a moon over the Teton mountains. The girl and I walked away from the camp fire. I knew what I was meant to do, I knew what I wanted to do, but something held me back. What if I tried to kiss her and she resisted me? The thought turned me into a stone. We walked back to the camp hand in hand, but that was as far as it went. I could have kicked myself for being such a poltroon, but if you've never kissed a girl before, it's a bit of an undertaking. In later life I've always maintained that if you hold hands with a girl and she returns your squeeze, you might just as well have slept with her. The intent is surely there. But this approach to the matter was not mine at the time, and I fretted all night in a sleeping bag under the starlit sky.

That pack trip was the windup of my camping days and I returned to Long Island for the fall season of dances—really big bashes—run either by Miss Juliana Cutting or a pair of ladies called Tappin and Tew. If you were on their lists you were asked to all the dances automatically, including the ones in town during the winter vacations.

Driving to a dance in the fall, I almost did myself in—out cold for two weeks. It was a matter of a high-crowned road in Syosset, a tree, and too much beer. When I came to in the hospital, the nurse handed me a clipping from the local paper. It was a brief write-up of my own demise. In this land of opportunity, that's one you don't often get.

A group of us from the Lawrence-Cedarhurst area used to convene at a roadhouse called Anthony's for a drink or two before driving across the Island. The parties were generally on the North Shore or in Westbury, where the very rich used to congregate. We were certainly not much of an asset to any party. We usually arrived half-crocked and immediately repaired to the bar, where we would stay most of the evening with others of our ilk. Girls didn't enter the picture much. A dance with the debutante maybe, if she were viable, then back to the bar again. Dawn would see most of us passed out under bushes with the soberest rounding us up for the drive home. Similarly, after a dance in New York, dawn would see us weaving homeward from the Plaza in top hat, white tie, and tails along the Park side of Fifth Avenue (with never a thought about being mugged).

Considering the expense our hosts went to—the long

driveways on Long Island lit by Japanese lanterns, Meyer Davis's orchestra, maybe an extra Marimba band, scrambled eggs and sausage catered by Louis Sherry, and the endless cases of champagne—we should have behaved more like little gentlemen and less like little swine. But the madcap drunk was much in vogue—Scott Fitzgerald bathing in the Plaza fountain, a decade earlier, had set a lasting tone.

In New York, we would gather at a speakeasy called Tony's in the East Fifties and consume buckets of a noxious drink called an Alexander, made of crème de cacao and brandy, which was said to be a powerful aphrodisiac. The stock market crashed about this time, but the dances went on undisturbed, as there always seemed to be someone around with money for this kind of thing. I remember one party at the Ritz, where the ballroom walls were draped in black satin and covered with white orchids. That was the year they were selling apples in the street.

My class at St. Paul's split roughly into thirds, one third each for Harvard, Yale, and Princeton, according to one's city of origin, Boston, New York, or Philadelphia. I chose Yale since New York was my base and it wasn't such a bad commute. My grandfather had gone to Yale and so had his uncle, Henry Barnard, who had a hall named after him on Hillhouse Avenue—a small building now housing the offices of Yale's Far Eastern publications. Henry, like Horace Mann in New York, reformed the public school systems of Connecticut and Rhode Island and became our first U.S. Commissioner of Education. Father had a great to-do with the president of Yale to ensure that the little building should be renamed Henry Barnard Hall, presumably to distinguish it from Barnard College named after a more distant cousin.

One of the first things I noticed about Yale was that all the squares from my class at St. Paul's immediately went to pieces. After the cloistered life there, exposure to the pleasures of drink and sex tends to corrupt the staunch. They had always lived by the rules, and when these were nonexistent, they failed to adjust as readily as we who had been breaking the rules all our lives. Many of the more outstanding members of my class at St. Paul's became hopeless drunks their freshman year at Yale. One or two never pulled out of it. This development was even more pronounced at Harvard where the attractions of Boston were only a step away. It's a pity that our educations coincide in time with so many other powerful distractions, such as learning about sex, drink, and now, drugs. Unless one is exceptionally bright or ambitious, getting an education comes off badly at this age. In my day drugs were no problem, but the opposite sex was a major preoccupation that far outweighed any academic interests.

My early attempts at seduction, it must be admitted, were all dismal failures. As a fledgling man-about-town, I asked a girl to the Yale-Princeton football game. She was blonde with a sly smile and big bosom—both features that had attracted me at some dance on Long Island. She accepted readily enough—her sly smile was ravishing—but on the special train to the game I felt something was definitely wrong. Conversation didn't flourish; she barely gave me the time of day when I modestly told her I used to play a bit at school. On the way into the stadium she chose a Princeton banner, which underlined my presentiments that the day was not going well. Every time Princeton made a gain, the wretched girl would leap to her feet cheering and waving like crazy. Yale never scored at all, but Princeton's final score read like a basketball tally. A bad day, but nothing compared to the evening that followed. The girl, unbeknownst to me, was in love with the center of the Princeton team to whose room we went for a victory celebration after the game. I felt out of place and out of sorts.

Not so Claribelle, or whatever her name was. She seemed to be on intimate terms with the whole Princeton team, while her oohings and aahings over this great lout of a center were an absolute revelation of the depths to which a woman can sink. I stood it for half an hour or so and then took an early train back to town, leaving her to her own devices. For all I know she returned to New York on their shoulders still waving her silly banner.

I played polo at Yale, but in order to play, you had to join the ROTC, which in those days was probably at its nadir. Today, some people get exicted about ROTC as a bad thing, but at that time nobody thought about war at all, or of the ROTC as anything but a bunch of harmless kooks. One summer the Yale and Harvard ROTC contingents spent six weeks in camp outside of Burlington, Vermont. Nearly everybody brought their own cars which made us a somewhat peculiar military unit, but that was the extent of motorization. We were a horsedrawn-artillery outfit, which even in those days was something of an anachronism. It took three pairs of horses to draw one French 75 or its accompanying caisson. With eight guns and eight caissons between the two batteries, there were more than a hundred horses (counting the spare mounts) to feed, water, and clean on the picket line. When it was my squad's turn at picket duty, rather than lugging the bales of hay on our backs, it seemed only logical to use my car to distribute the hay. Consequently, we loaded the bales in the rumble seat, and I drove slowly along the picket line while they pitched them out at appropriate intervals. We got the job done in half the time, but it was considered most unmilitary. From then on I was a marked man, a troublemaker.

Presumably, if it hadn't been for this incident, I would have been spared the humiliation of being caught feigning a bad toe. While my squad was out on KP or some other disagreeable task, I was found lying on my cot reading a magazine. An insufferable square from the Harvard group marched into my tent, ripped the adhesive tape off my uninjured toe, and threatened court-martial proceedings. I considered his action an invasion of privacy, but decided not to press it. My cousin was captain pro tem of the camp because in New Haven he once gave a pair of ducks and some theater tickets to the Army captain in charge. When I was brought up before the two of them, family ties prevailed and I was let off with a reprimand much to the disgust of the character from Harvard. I'm sure that he later distinguished himself in World War II for devotion to duty and attention to detail.

Our second year at Yale four of us did a lot of table tipping. When others played bridge, we communed with the infinite. Our favorite spirit was Conan Doyle, who always seemed to be hanging around with powerful emanations. We tested him once by putting a glass on a table on the other side of the room and asking him if he could knock it off. He rapped out a definite "yes," but we did have to move the glass to the edge of the table, at which point, of course, it fell off.

One of our friends at school had died the previous summer, and with some trepidation we got in touch with him one night. Almost at once the table took off on its own. The message was loud and clear: "Stop this, or you will go out of your minds!" We stopped. I'm no nut on the subject, but I will point out that if any of our foursome was moving the table with his leg the joke would have worn pretty thin after a week or so. We did rub our hands on our trousers to generate electricity, and one leg of the table was propped up on a book to make the rapping easier. Nevertheless, there is something there—call it what you will.

My club at Yale was Psi Upsilon, later the Fence Club, known by some as "Harvard in Yale" after the terminology of the missionary endeavor, Yale in China. (We also had a

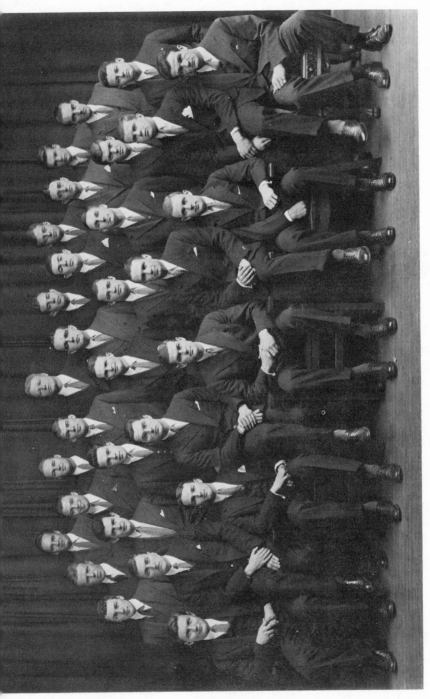

Psi Upsilon (now The Fence Club) Yale Class of '34 (J.L.B. second row, second from left)

Yale in Hartford—the Chemistry Lab, way out on Whitney Avenue.) In my day there was a great deal of mumbo jumbo attendant on election to a fraternity. There were three good ones, three intermediate, and one bad one. I was under considerable pressure to be elected to Psi Upsilon, one of the good ones, as Father had been a Psi U man at Columbia and was very keen that I should follow in his footsteps. So as not to seem too keen myself, my reaction, whenever I saw a member walking down the street in New Haven was to cross to the other side in order to avoid him. The big night came in the early fall when the membership of each fraternity put on Ku Klux Klan type robes and tramped around the campus in double file with torches, chanting their marching songs. The lyrics of these were simple stuff, two favorites being "Psi U, my ass to you," and "We will pull the chain on Alpha Delta Phi." It was fun and rather silly after you were elected, but beforehand it was eerie, and even disconcerting—all those shuffling peers weighing one in the balance.

The fraternities were primarily eating clubs, and before I became a member, a group of us used to have our meals in a restaurant on the first floor of an old New England boarding-house. One of the waitresses, a daughter of the house, was a little star—black hair, black eyes, always smiling, and stacked. As she wanted to be an actress, it seemed only kind to do something for her, so on her day off I asked her to come to the theater with me in New York. I suppose in the back of my mind I envisaged a wild night of passion at the Waldorf, but as it turned out we went down in the afternoon, saw *Design for Living*, and returned that same evening on the milk train. After the show we had gone to Tony's where I plied her with Alexanders. It was a long day's journey into night. Far from having the desired effect, the Alexanders acted like so much aspirin. She slept the sleep of the innocent all the way back to New Haven.

I did better with a girl I met that summer coming home on a boat from Europe. I first saw her walking up the gangplank. It was the year that Princess Eugénie hats were the fashion. Her Eugénie hat was not quite right, and my heart went out to her. Ordinarily you never see any shipboard acquaintance again, but we were the exception. We saw each other constantly, every weekend in New York, and we became, as the story books say, very much in love. Then a viper stole into our paradise in the form of the man she had left behind in Europe. I couldn't believe he existed at first since he didn't seem to hamper our relationship. The more she mentioned her fiancé, the more I thought he was just a myth to keep me on my toes. When she produced pictures of some sleazy jerk, I began to falter a bit, but dismissed them as probably her brother. Whoever he was didn't seem to matter. Our passion progressed quite naturally to the inevitable bedding down. I remember going home that night on a sort of simulated Cloud Nine. It hadn't really been that great, but I felt that now I could die a happy man having experienced all. My bliss, if you can call it that, was short-lived. The following day my love and I were having a picnic in Central Park. The dialogue ran as follows—

"Darling?" She was very solemn.

"Yes."

"You know I hate to say this . . ."

"Say what?"

"Well . . . it's just that now I know I don't love you. You see, last night you didn't make me come."

Her fiancé, who presumably did, arrived on these shores the next week. They were married shortly thereafter with a large reception at the Colony Club. I had taken to my bed with a fever which soared when, on the day of her wedding, she came to see me and Mother wouldn't let her in the house. There's nothing like a raging fever to still the pangs of jealousy.

Emotion is foreign to a great many WASPs who consider indulgence therein too Latin, but I was new at the
game and the thought of "my love" repeating *our* intima-
cies with another so shook me that I was physically ill.
Looking back on this first affair, I can see now that it had
a lasting effect on me. It was the first time I had given myself trustingly to another, nothing at all held back, and the
results were most painful. I felt rejected, inadequate and
totally alone. Very unpleasant sensations, certainly not to
be repeated. I resolved then and there never to expose myself again.

Following this dismal ending to what had been an all-
consuming interest, I took up with a girl who also was
recovering from an unfortunate love affair. She was one of
those young women, of whom there are many, who love to
mother drunks. Now I like drinking, but I've never been a
real drunk—the kind of fellow who needs a hair of the dog
the morning after. We were, therefore, not made for one
another, but we enjoyed each other's company. Despite my
resolve, we made some halfhearted attempts to get emotionally involved, but there was no chemistry and every
time we lay down on a couch together we would burst out
laughing. It's extraordinary how lethal laughter is to lovemaking, but you can't do much in bed if you're doubled up
with mirth.

Her Prince Charming came along that summer in the
person of John O'Hara, who at that time was involved in
the musical production of his *Pal Joey* stories. Drinking
heavily then, he was in constant need of wet towels on his
forehead, countless cups of coffee, and perhaps a scrambled egg in the small hours of the morning. In short, he was
absolute grist for her mill. I used to take her out to dinner
and the movies and end up at the Stork Club where we
would sit at the bar waiting for John to appear. He would
show up around one o'clock, drunk as a lord and complete-

ly unintelligible, but you only had to look in her eyes to see that love light shining. I wondered if anyone would ever beam that look at me.

My courses at Yale were chosen with one desideratum in mind, namely that they not interfere with my weekends. That meant only one or two classes on Friday morning and maybe another on Monday afternoon which required no preparation. Selecting courses to meet these goals led to some strange pockets of learning, such as "American Silver" and "Pre-Raphaelite Painters," in both of which I excelled. "Roman Band Instruments" was an old favorite, but that was before my time. We had one splendid course called "Gentlemen's Chemistry" that met on Thursdays in the afternoon. A Professor Timms was the lecturer, and he really knew his audience. There was a laboratory sink and counter on a big stage, and each week he would put on a sort of magic show with smoking test tubes and indecent-looking bottles, accompanying his demonstrations with a merry prattle. Everybody loved it. Occasionally we would have written tests, at which point he would leave the room, closing the door behind him. At the end of fifteen minutes, he would return, hammer on the door, and shout through it that we could now put our books away. You can have faith in a man like that. One unfortunate youth had such faith in Professor Timms that he brought down the house one day when, in a question and answer period, he asked in a piping voice whether masturbation brought on pimples. As he was seated well to the back of the room, the entire class wheeled around to view the questioner and burst into loud guffaws on seeing his ravaged face. The Professor was kinder, and after putting the poor wretch's mind at ease, pointed out to the rest of us that scientific inquiry was what his course was all about.

I studied a great deal of Spanish and French at college. I got started on Spanish because Father thought it would be useful to me in a business career in Latin America. Nothing could have been further from my thoughts. Still, Spanish was an easy language and we read a lot of novels by Blasco-Ibanez and Pepe Jiminez and, of course, Cervantes. The only thing I remember from several years of this are two quotes from Ibanez, which I'm glad to say have enriched my life considerably. The first is from *Blood and Sand*, which closes with the gored matador being carried out of the ring while the crowd roars. The last line of the book is "La fiera rugia (the beast roared), la unica, la verdadera" (the only one, the true one). The other is from *Mare Nostrum*. A pair of lovers are wandering around the aquarium in Naples. They stop in front of a tank housing some codlike fish that noses up to the glass, displaying a huge underlip. The girl turns her face to the man and murmurs "Quisiera (I would like) un beso (kiss) stupendo." Neither line is much use in international finance, but I find them rewarding nevertheless.

French is a language that basically escapes me and I've been exposed to a lot of it in one form or another, ranging from *Babar* as a child to an advanced seminar on Molière in my senior year at Yale. I have never been able to think in French and to the French this is inexcusable. The only time I thought like a Frenchman was in a situation that was something like a Feydeau farce. I was in competition with a sleek Gallic type for the favors of an older woman in New York. The lady had a suite in one of the big hotels, and I had a late date with her one Saturday night, after she returned from a dinner. When I arrived for my tryst the door was open so I tiptoed down the hall to her bedroom. Here again the door was ajar, but from inside came a rhythmic pumping noise. I froze. Obviously that wretched Frenchman had beaten me to the draw. I listened in fascination. On and on went the rhythmic pumping and even what sounded like an occasional sigh of pleasure. My admiration for the French began to reach new heights. And yet there was something wrong. No man could go on that long, especially with the lady in question. Summoning courage I pushed open the door and gazed on an empty bed. The radiator was pumping away like something crazy with occasional sighs of steam.

There was another girl about this time who was a passionate Catholic, and I use the adjective advisedly. After a night of passion she would be consumed by intense remorse and we would have to go to church together to get rid of her burden of sin. Normally, I gather, people whisper those things into the confessional, but not so this one. Once as we were walking down the aisle, to my horror, she suddenly dropped to her knees, then stretched out full-length the way the Cardinals do at the elevation of a Pope and beat her head on the stone floor. Well, you can imagine my reaction. I slunk into a nearby pew, avoiding all the upturned eyes, and fumbled through a Bible searching for Ezekiel 23.

I mention these ladies, not out of any desire to be salacious, but because the opposite sex holds at least equal rank with college as an influence in my formative years. After all, women play a big part in a man's life and we are not told much about them. In addition to her capabilities in bed, my Catholic girl friend had a marvelous sense of the drama of history, which she made much more interesting than any professor I can remember. We used to recite together G. K. Chesterton's *Battle of Lepanto.*

> The cold queen of England is staring in the glass;
> The shadow of the Valois is yawning at the mass;
> From evening isles fantastical rings faint the Spanish
> gun
> And the Lord upon the Golden Horn is laughing in the
> sun.

The sweep of history is there, and from those four lines

whole story of Europe, the Middle East and the New World. She would give me a hundred to one that I couldn't give the name and number of that "shadow of the Valois." It's Charles IX, a son of Catherine de Medici and Henry II. I learned the hard way.

Looking back, it is shocking to consider how much education was offered on a platter at Yale and how little any of us took. We were the element in our generation that led President Conant of Harvard to say a few years later that "the primary purpose of education is not the development of an appreciation of 'the good life' in young gentlemen born to the purple." Conant was talking about the pleasures of luxury, but if we eliminate the born-to-the-purple bit and extend the "good life" concept to take in cultural pleasures, it seems to me that is exactly what education should be—a reservoir of enjoyment for life.

Father's advice was "Graduate, boy . . . that's all that matters." To this end my courses had been chosen with care. What they fitted me for in the real world was another question.

CHAPTER

3

In my day, after graduation the majority went in for business or the professions. Only the oddballs took up science or religion. That still left a few lazy slobs who, for want of anything better, gravitated to self-expression. I was one of the latter. Briefly the idea of a corporate career flitted through my mind, but then I never understood how anyone could get passionately interested in panty hose or any other product. We slow maturers are penalized. A friend, who at one point during the war was enjoying Pensacola, used to ask why nobody had told him before about the Navy Air Force. Schools should provide the young with a daily pitch, exposing them to the allure of a wide variety of subjects from Architecture to Zoology. If they did, a now miserable poet or painter might be a happy mortician. As it was I planned to be a writer. My qualifications were minimal to say the least. An A in a Daily Theme course wasn't much to go on, but you've got to start somewhere. Besides I had the writer's temperament. I knew this because I began sharpening pencils, quite elaborate ones. Before committing anything to paper, I felt I should broaden my outlook. After graduation, therefore, I embarked on a six month trip around the world to gain the needed perspective.

My first stop was Cairo, Egypt, where I made some essential purchases—a solar topee and a fly whisk. I also acquired a dragoman. I don't know whether dragomen still exist, but in those days they did everything. My man's name was Ali Shahat Abed, and from the moment he signed on I didn't have to lift a finger. My general plan was to take the train to Assuan where I would hire a boat to sail down the Nile past Luxor, Thebes, the Valley of the Kings, and back to Cairo. The overnight trip to Assuan was memorable, primarily because I had Gyppy tummy and everytime I went to the john, a dirty little hole on the train, I had to step over several recumbent figures. We got quite chummy as the evening progressed.

The boat was a felucca rig with a crew of five in addition to me and Ali. Its LOA was about twenty feet. Ali and I sat in the stern sheets, and the crew, all five of them, lived on the foredeck. Sailing, as I've explained, was not my strong point, but never have I seen such abysmal seamen as this lot. The moment the wind blew about five knots they lowered the sail. As a result we drifted down the Nile, mostly backwards, and it took a good two weeks.

Throughout, Ali Shahat Abed was magnificent. He was not only a well-informed guide and chancellor of the exchequer, but a superb cook and body servant extraordinary. One night we tied up at a primitive dock on the banks of the Nile and I went ashore to explore the village. It was a rather unfriendly place, peopled with dark shadows and unpleasant characters and I decided to leave. It was some way back to the boat and en route I sensed this shadow behind me. I didn't want to show panic so I kept on at the same pace and the shadow kept pace with me. Finally I got back to the friendly lights of the boat and turned to face my pursuer. It was Ali, of course, who had been watching and warding the whole time. This was man-to-man stuff and my heart went out to him.

Conditions along the banks of the Nile were really primitive. Water to irrigate the farms was still being pumped by methods used in the days of Abraham. A donkey prodded by a small boy with a switch was hitched up to a large wooden wheel with its axle sunk in the ground. The boy and donkey walked around the wheel in an endless circle, thereby turning it, and slowly the water flowed. "Mahound was in his paradise, above the evening star"—that is to say Farouk was thumbing through his "feelthy pictures" in Cairo and not paying much attention to the plight of the fellaheen. Probably he figured they had been doing this kind of thing for quite a few millennia and a few more wouldn't hurt.

One night Ali produced a sheik of the desert for me. He was presumably a brother of Ali's, but then Ali had brothers everywhere. We were tied up to another little primitive dock when the brother and three other men on horseback suddenly appeared on the bank above us. The stars were shining with desert brightness, and the men were swathed in black from head to toe. The air was charged with drama. I had told Ali that I wanted to get a really good scarab as a present for my father, so by the light of a deck lantern Ali's brother laid out a black velvet cloth against which the multicolored scarabs gleamed in splendor. He looked just like those Assyrian types we used to play football against in Central Park. I chose a scarab of a deep liverish hue that he swore by Allah had come from Tutankhamen's tomb. As he certainly looked like a man who would have illegal access to a tomb, I parted with one hundred dollars. We all shook hands on the deal, and they swept off into the night.

The next day I felt I had been had, and when we got back to Cairo, I took the scarab to several good jewelers and even to Professor Breasted's office in the Egyptian Museum in an effort to determine whether or not it was authentic. They all chipped away with special chisels and hammers, but nobody could make a scratch on it. This was no proof of anything, of course, but together with my faith in Ali, I was satisfied. Unfortunately, I had it mounted on a cheap gold stick pin, which made it look like nothing at all. Father wore it once and then popped it into his jewel box from which it never emerged. Our relations were always like that—much thought about the other on both sides, and no contact.

Leaving Egypt, I took off for India in a huge four-motored biplane that must have been a relic of World War I. With much creaking and straining of struts, it lumbered into the air like an old buzzard and literally seemed to flap its wings as we flew. After two harrowing days on this "tetradactyl," which served as a mail plane for various Beau Geste-type forts in the desert, we finally reached Bombay.

My first impression of the subcontinent was that my solar topee was wrong. It was the kind worn by Stanley when he was looking for Dr. Livingstone. Large and white and with a long overhang in back, it looked very out of place when compared with the neat little tan ones put out by Lock and favored by representatives of the British raj.

Bombay I remember because of its "Towers of Silence" erected by the Parsees, those descendants of Persian Zoroastrians who fled to India in the seventh century to escape Moslem persecution. The top floor of a tower is open to the elements and is laid out in a slightly concave, wheel-shaped design, with shallow drainage canals where the spokes of the wheel should be. When a good Parsee dies, the body is laid out on one of these spokes. The vultures and the sun do the rest. The rains come and whatever is left over, which isn't much, is washed down a central hole in the middle. Parochially, I had always thought of "dust unto dust returning" as an exclusively Christian concept. This is not a moral book, but an argument could be made that insofar as you are honest and live by reasonably decent rules, there is somewhere a force for good. Zoroas-

Wrong solar topee

trians maintain that this force is in a cosmic struggle with a force for evil. It could be—there are a lot of baddies around—but it seems too much of a comic-strip plot for a concept so great as the cosmos.

A haze suffuses India, smelling of dung and curry, under which the Indians amuse themselves as best they can, reproducing their kind in geometric progression. When I was there, the princely states were still in existence—there was Udaipur, the gates of its great palace guarded by caparisoned elephants and, out on a scenic lake, the Maharajah's summer palace, which could be reached by Victorian launch. Jaipur I remember principally for the non-purchase of a large brass plate, the kind you now see made into coffee tables in dubious bachelor studies. The delicate tracery of its design, made up of tiny red, blue and yellow parakeets perched in lacework trees, was superb, but the plate was heavy and I made, I thought, a sensible decision. Rather than lug it across India, I would pick one up on the other side in Calcutta. I was wrong, because the ones in Calcutta didn't compare in quality. I began to realize that India didn't go in for outlets throughout the country and central distribution.

Srinagar, the capital of Kashmir, used to be a watering place for members of the British raj escaping the summer heat. Set in a fertile valley at the base of the Karakoram range, the town with its great overhanging houses on either side of the river Jhelum had the appearance of a disorganized, gargantuan Bruges. Just outside town, reached by a poplared road, the Dal Lake made a placid pleasance of ducks and lotus blossoms on the border of which were a row of dingy houseboats. I had rented one of these in New York through Thomas Cook and Son. Lately, I gather, the place has become quite garish, what with war and tourism, but in those days it was quiet and gentle and rather run-down colonial.

Checking in at the local Cook office, a tiny one-room affair reminiscent of a stamp dealer's emporium, I was greeted by a mustachioed English Army type in tan shorts, tan bush jacket, and tan solar topee. Fortunately, my own white Stanley model had been jettisoned by then, so I felt more on an equal footing with the "major." A merry type, I sensed a kindred spirit as he drove me to the houseboat. Rattling along in his dilapidated Bentley (one door was tied on with string), he described the domestic arrangements. "Your number one boy, the majordomo as it were . . . Philosophic chap, calls himself Radakrishna . . . Drives some people to drink. Whoa!" he said, narrowly missing a cow on the road, "*that* would never do. Doesn't touch it himself," he continued, "and there's plenty of it on board. I see to that end personally." We had "elevenses" in the form of a gin and tonic on the afterdeck in the shade, and he departed with the cryptic words, "My wife will be here at five to take you to the club. Don't be surprised when you see her."

The houseboat had a staff of six, not including two men who sat in a punt by the side of the road and whose only job was to paddle me out some twenty yards to the boat and then back again whenever I wanted to leave. It had a largish salon with wicker chairs, English hunting prints, and a profusion of Indian rugs. In addition there was a good-sized dining room and two bedrooms, and on top of the boat was a verandah with more wicker chairs and an awning. The whole deal, including staff, food and a well-stocked cellar, was one hundred dollars a week.

The major's wife appeared at five without the major and she was indeed remarkable—coal black and swathed in a purple sari. The effect was dramatic. She was no beauty by normal standards, but distinguished looking and spoke perfect Oxford English. We had a drink on the verandah before taking off for the club.

Houseboat staff—Radakrishna on my left

This club was right out of Kipling—mess jackets, turbaned waiters, God-save-the-King all the way. Our arrival seemed to cause quite a few tribal eyebrows to raise, but then we were an *outré* pair to be invading the inner sanctum, a coal black woman and a transatlantic type who was probably carrying a gun. I gathered later that non-whites were rigidly excluded from the club, but an exception had been made for the major's wife because she was a daughter of the Maharajah.

The major, who managed the club as well as Thomas Cook and Son, greeted us affably and took us to a table that was somewhat apart from the others. Already seated at the table, and slightly tipsy, were a Scotch botanist and his wife. The table, the major explained, was one they kept reserved for transients, who usually had a better time at it than the regular members did at theirs. I wondered whether the major was being tactful because we were in some form of Coventry. It soon became apparent that the major himself was an outcast for having married a non-white. She, in turn, was not recognized at the palace for having married the major. Somehow this bond between us all did make for a merry and quite cohesive table. The botanist was one of those free spirits who just didn't give a damn.

Outside the club confines, our little band of outcasts was joined by a Rajput captain and a low caste industrialist from Agra, both clients of the major. The captain was a dashing fellow with a close-cropped military moustache, dark olive complexion, and a smile of very white teeth. The industrialist looked like a smaller version of the botanist with glasses; both wore sloppy seersucker suits and open-neck shirts and looked as if they were about to take the subway to Coney Island. We all drank together on the houseboat, took picnics around the countryside, and enjoyed each other immensely.

One of our junkets was to Gulmarg, an embryonic golf course and a few houses in the foothills of the Himalayas. Gulmarg then was very remote. The final stage of the trip was by pony up a steep mountain trail. En route, one is meant to catch a glimpse of K-2, the second highest peak in the Himalayas, but the day we did it everything was shrouded in mist. We were greeted at the top by a Major Lamb who seemed delighted to see us and took us to his house for a drink. He and his wife were types that could only exist in the British colonial empire. She hooked rugs out of llama wool in the long winter evenings and his chief claim to fame was a boiled egg, a Lamb egg as he called it, the secret of which was a lot of Worcestershire sauce and a liberal shot of brandy. How he and our own major ever acquired their military rank crossed my mind fleetingly, but I dismissed the thought as unworthy. Both had a puckish attitude toward life that made the world their oyster. I suppose they were working for MI-5.

Raffles Hotel in Singapore was a sprawling Victorian wooden structure that gave off a romantic aura of spies and counterspies. You felt intrigue behind every palm. I had invited the captain of an American schooner to dine because he had advertised in the local paper that he had a berth and was headed for Java. The next scheduled boat for Java required a wait of ten days. The seventy-foot schooner was one of those boats that takes a group of college dropouts on a round-the-world voyage and presumably makes men and women out of them by exposing them to the hazards of the sea. As there were no paid hands on board and a great many weak links, the hazards were not to be sneezed at. On a scale of ten for effectiveness, the captain and his mate would score ten and the fourteen others in the crew ranged from zero to one.

Our second night out we ran into what I considered a typhoon—great waves crashing over the deck, a torn mainsail, people throwing up in the main cabin, and the two effectives howling for joy on the poop deck. The following day the storm had passed, the sun emerged, and the sea calmed down to a gentle blue. We set a great square-rigged sail to catch the following wind and progressed for two days in what amounted to a sailor's paradise, reading, tying knots and just lazing about in the sun. I remember climbing up into the crow's nest and watching for hours a school of sea turtles playing around the ship. Merry characters, the sea turtles seemed to be smiling and were enjoying life to the full, totally unaware that they had become commercially valuable.

We went ashore in Sumatra with the idea of shooting a tiger. As only the two effectives had heavy weapons, while the rest of us carried .22s, it was just as well we never saw a tiger. One of our girl dropouts, an unfortunate type with a speech impediment and no redeeming features whatever, kept seeing "thnakes" on our tramp through the jungle. I'm not very good about snakes. Frankly, I found her alarms unnerving, particularly since it seemed to me we were deep in their natural habitat. That old movie shot where the python drops out of a tree never left me for a moment. All in all, you can have the jungles of Sumatra. I prefer walking on Madison Avenue or Bond Street with a tightly rolled umbrella.

One night we threw an anchor on the side of Krakatoa, the volcano that blew up in 1883 and whose ashes were said to have fallen in London eight thousand miles away. Somehow looking down on a lake of seething lava makes one realize what a miserable underpinning our biosphere really has and what small wonder it is that we don't blow up entirely. Ever since *The Last Days of Pompeii*, volcanoes have added a certain extra quality to whatever is going on. People who live on Stromboli view life differently from those who live on Pook's Hill.

Our schooner tied up in Batavia now called Jakarta, and

eight of the male crew members headed for town that evening, leaving the captain and the first mate to look after
the ladies on board. As our ship carried no drink except for
medicinal purposes, once ashore, we reacted in the time-
honored tradition of the American Navy and headed for
the nearest gin palace. This turned out to be a "very nice
place" in the native quarter, just outside of town. A taxi
driver, grumbling all the way at the size of our group, described it as such and said we would enjoy it.

The nice place turned out to be an enormous brothel laid
out scientifically in a sort of compound. On the street
where we pulled up, there was a long, low building which
served as a dance hall, bar, and short-order restaurant.
Stretching out behind this building at right angles to it
were four or five rows of one-story shacks facing each other,
each row separated by an alley. The shacks were all identical, consisting of a roofed front porch with a bedroom separated from the porch area by a colored bead curtain.
There must have been at least a hundred of these units in
the compound.

Our group settled down at a table in the dance hall and
ordered a round of beer. It was good Dutch beer, and after
we'd had three or four, our attention, as it will under these
circumstances, began to focus on forks and spoons and our
more immediate surroundings. Beyond these, the dance
hall swayed and blared in an indeterminate haze. Directly
in front of our table making eyes at us while dancing with
another girl was a sinuous Indonesian in a tight-fitting, red
satin dress. She was also wearing gold-rimmed spectacles,
normally not a sex symbol, but her movements were such,
both in front and behind, that only the most captious
would consider the glasses a detriment. Certainly none of
us did. She joined us, of course, with her friend, but the
latter must have sensed the competition and drifted away
to greener fields leaving the eight of us in charge of this

pearl of the Orient. We were certainly a loutish group, but then everybody was so busy staring down her front that there was no one left to carry the conversational ball. The girl just giggled happily, obviously operating on the theory that one man's leer is as good as another's.

"Come," she said after a few of us had a fling at dancing, or rather holding on as she gyrated, "I like American boys. One guilder each," she stated her price. "Eight guilders, please, the lot."

Stumbling down the alley to her quarters, we ran into other nationalities stumbling back—Poles, Germans, Swedes, and Lascars, the one true League of Nations where everybody's interests are the same. Most of the shacks were dark as the evening was still young, and their occupants were busy in the dance hall. Once at her shack, she turned on the light behind the bead curtain and stepped out of her red satin dress. The rest of us shuffled about like so many sheep on the porch.

"I'm ready, please," she said, parting the beads with her bosom.

Not being a group of potential leaders, nobody made a move. It was much like that line in *Horatius at the Bridge* where ". . . those behind cried 'Forward!' And those before cried 'Back!'" We ended it by shoving the youngest, not much more than a cabin boy, into the lion's den and sat down on the porch to wait.

The bead curtain, of course, provided next to no privacy and every sound could be heard. The girl put on a terrific show, much moaning and groaning punctuated by squeals of ecstasy, that could scarcely be attributed to the prowess of the cabin boy. In little groups of twos and threes we all eventually ended up in the bedroom and took our minor parts in the production, a nipple here, a buttock there, while awaiting the stellar role. The girl throughout was rolling her eyes and pounding the bed with her hands in what we all concluded afterwards must have been the real thing. There was, however, an element of doubt, for when the last man had spent himself, she suddenly sat up in bed and asked for her glasses which had rolled to the floor. Putting them on, she glanced at her watch.

"Eight guilders, please," she said. "I go back now dancing."

I didn't know what to expect of China, but certainly not what I found. First of all, in my mind's eye I had pictured China as a warm place with lotus blossoms, long-bearded sages, and delicate parasolled ladies drinking tea in a summer house. Instead, when I got to Peking, it was bitterly cold and all the Chinese were bundled up in padded blue quilts. Instead of lotus blossoms, the land was a barren waste, as if they had been strip mining it since the Han dynasty. Outside of Peking, the landscape was made even bleaker by antlike files of soldiers that covered the countryside on their shaggy Manchurian ponies, the latter so small that it looked as though the soldiers could put their feet on the ground and let the ponies walk out from under them. It was the year of "the Long March" when Mao led the Communist army from Kiangsi to Yenan, but the event was then too current to make any impression on me. Milestones are like that. I know if I'd been in Jerusalem at the time of the crucifixion I wouldn't have noticed a thing.

Politics have never been my cup of tea. To mix a metaphor, ikons made of men's hope for liberty too often have feet of clay. My interests in China were primarily porcelain and jade and trying to get a grasp on past Chinese history. In the latter effort I did quite well, managing to boil down the Chinese dynasties to only six that need be remembered. To my thinking a dynasty has to last at least two hundred fifty years in order to qualify. You can't have a dynasty with just a couple of generations, but Sinologists, by forever misusing this splendid word, have needlessly added confusion to what in effect is fairly straightforward stuff. Applying my ground rules, Chinese dynastic history goes like this—all you have to think of is Chou and Han followed by chaos; then Tang and Sung separated from Ming and Ching by Kublai Khan, and you've got the thing in a nutshell. Modern China and I grew up together, very separate and rather unequal. Unfortunately, I won't be around to judge whether Mao's successors achieve dynastic status. They won't be eligible until 2200 A.D.

The teachings of Mao have, I know, great current appeal, but at the risk of seeming unregenerate, they strike me as a little drab when compared with a Ming vase *famille rose* or a pottery horse of the Tang period. It may be because the past for me has more fascination than the present. Of course you are stuck with the present for better or for worse, but you can adopt from the past any epoch in a country's history the connotations of which appeal to you— eighteenth-century England, seventeenth-century France, Renaissance Italy, and so on. Applying this principle to China, I would select the twelfth-century southern Sung dynasty, which had its capital at Hangchow, the southern terminus of the Grand Canal. It was there, I have realized, that my image of China was born. The southern Sung enjoyed a long era of relative peace, and Hangchow was able to develop a style of "gracious living" along with a burgeoning of the arts in general, and landscape painting in particular. Today the mountains still circle Lake Si in beauty, the lotus blossoms fall, but all other signs of this gentle capital are gone, gratuitously demolished during the Taiping rebellion. The town is now a shipping center.

The moment I got on the Inland Sea in Japan, I should have known there was trouble brewing. Each day of the voyage to Yodo at its eastern end, the purser of our small steamship, who was Japanese, turned on his radio full volume at 5:00 P.M. and listened to a program of bugle calls. Apparently the literature of bugle calls in Japan was extensive, and the purser was kept quite busy writing descriptive notes on a small pad in his office. From time to time there would be a sad series of notes on the bugle, and the purser would shake his head dejectedly. "Retreat," he explained. "Very bad." Then his glasses would gleam as the bugle changed its tune. "Banzai! Charge!" he shouted, getting into the spirit of the thing and threatening me with his pencil. Obviously, the spirit of his ancestors was moving in him and like a *dummkopf* I merely thought that the purser was off his rocker. It was five years before Pearl Harbor.

My immediate destination was Kyoto, the capital of Japan until 1868 and its cultural center for centuries. Think of a vast Oriental flea market purveying cloisonné, bronzes, porcelains, and lacquer and you have the essence of Kyoto. Curiously enough Kyoto was the one major city in Japan to escape American bombing during World War II and today, despite an industrial overlay, still maintains much of its earlier character of parks and gardens in addition to the myriad shops. When I was there, except for big industrial centers like Osaka and the Tokyo-Yokohama complex, all Japan seemed a garden, much like the miniatures reproduced in gravel-filled bowls in a florist's window.

Just outside of Kyoto there is a short, rushing river where you could take a boat and, placing yourself in the hands of the Japanese boatmen, shoot the rapids. The borders of the river on either side go straight up in steep forested slopes of fir and pine, with occasional outcroppings of rock on which you might expect to see perched a crane or a torii gate. The intimacy of the Japanese landscape is lost for a moment in the swirl and dip of the boat as the current takes hold with a sudden surge and apparent disaster is warded off by the long poles of the shouting boatmen in their round straw hats. The scene is straight Hokusai or Hiroshige Ando, those two simplistic landscape painters who developed wood engraving in color to such an individualized art in the mid-nineteenth century.

In Kyoto, I stayed at the Imperial Hotel, which in itself was an education in the Japanese scene. One day at lunch there was some sort of a male gala going on in a private room off the main dining room. Pompously dressed in striped trousers, morning coats and top hats, the invitees traversed the main dining room en route to this private retreat. Whatever they were serving inside, it must have been considerably more than saki, because the effect on the guests was overwhelming. Over coffee I watched in fascination as the first one was carried out, feet first and stiff as a board, with his coat tails trailing and his top hat neatly placed on his stomach. A few minutes later two more emerged in the same fashion. Of course, maybe they had been poisoned—you never know East of Suez—but I think it was an import known as whiskey-soda, probably without the soda.

After lunch I took a short stroll in the adjacent gardens, which were carved out of the hillside behind the hotel. A neat gravelled walk wound between gnarled trees, a little stream, and what looked like Buddhist shrines in stone until it reached a point almost at the top of the hill. There to my astonishment I came upon a man, stark naked, standing under an icy waterfall, chattering and shouting what must have been prayers of penance. Discreetly I turned back to the hotel. The old and the new in Japan were then very much in juxtaposition.

The Japanese differ from the Chinese in that the Chinese today are motivated by a discipline that is both egalitarian and puritanical, and the Japanese most definitely are not. We in the West aren't either, of course, but there the similarity ends. Despite their apparent westernization, I can't help feeling that there is a dark side to the Japanese character, the kamikaze side, that has been bred into them over a thousand years of violence. The civilizing effect of Zen Buddhism, for instance, is all very well for a few aesthetes, but the Bushido code of the samurai was ingrained in that purser on the boat. Karate, too, is an off-putting thing. I simply don't feel at ease with a man who may kick me in the Adam's apple or split a brick with his head.

Japanese women, however, are absolutely tops. I remember buying an umbrella from a doll-like creature on the street. The umbrella was made of oiled paper spread on bamboo struts and cost about one yen, but during the whole transaction the girl treated me like the Emperor Meiji himself. Wreathed in smiles, she dropped to her knees and presented the umbrella with outstretched arms as if it had been made of the finest silks and ivory. It made me feel very crass producing a coin to pay for it.

My last evening in Japan was spent in a lavish house of ill-repute. I was ushered into a downstairs private dining room for dinner. The decor was simple, mats on the floor, sliding paper doors, a round, low-slung table, and a small alcove with a delicate scroll painting in it. The alcove is known as the *takonoma,* the place in a room where the Japanese display their finest works of art. These are placed in the alcove one at a time so that they may be savored to the full and are changed on a rotating basis once a week, or once a month, depending on the owner's supply. Unfortunately I had mistaken the *takonoma* for a place to throw my overcoat, but with much goodwill on both sides this cultural shock was absorbed and I proceeded to order the meal—eels tempora and a beef sukiyaki.

The dinner was well-done in the best Oriental style. A geisha girl, quite lovely but aloof, crouched in one corner providing background music on a lutelike instrument. The meal itself was cooked on a low table in front of me by what looked like identical twins in pink kimonos, who hovered about pouring the hot saki wine and smiling over each mouthful of food, which was literally hand-fed. The meal, I must say, was delicious. Following it, I collapsed on cushions specially provided for the barbarian back while the sisters applied moist towels to my face and accompanied their ministrations with soft cooing murmurs. Since these were in their native tongue, they might well have been saying "you filthy swine" for all I know, but if they were, I couldn't tell it by the tone of their voices.

The lute girl left just as I seemed to be dropping off. I watched her out of half-closed eyelids. As she went out she bowed very low, backing out of the door. She was in a different category of endeavor.

I must have dozed a minute or two, maybe more, because when I awoke I was alone with one of the twins. She was lying beside me smiling.

"You sleep," she said, stating the fact. I started to say something, but she gently placed her little fingers on my lips. "We go," she said, "my room is just upstairs."

I have always maintained that the chemistry of mutual sexual attraction is unpremeditated, swift, silent, and special—and thoroughly understood by both parties. In the present instance, of course, there was considerable premeditation, but at the same time the chemistry was there.

When we got to her room, however, I was totally unprepared for what greeted me. She opened the door and turned on a switch that made the room quite bright and also turned on the phonograph. I stood in the doorway transfixed. The room was a shrine to Gary Cooper!

Four large close-ups of his stalwart face smiled out at me from her dressing table. Several more adorned the walls along with a life-size poster of the star striding across a corral. There was even a western hat on the bed, which gave

the impression he had just stepped out for a pack of cigarettes. Now I've always admired Gary Cooper, but at this
particular juncture I felt his presence inhibiting.

My companion by then had nothing on but her panties,
and her arms were around my shoulders drawing me into a
dance. She was looking at me tenderly.

"You no like?" she asked.

"Oh yes . . . splendid," I said.

"Maybe too much light?"

I nodded.

Obediently she disengaged herself and flicked off the
wall switch. The phonograph ground to a discordant stop,
which was too bad, but the pictures receded in the half-
light. As we sank to the bed together, I managed to kick
the hat onto the floor, which made me feel things were
looking up.

If one takes the view that travel is a broadening experience, did this "grand tour" of mine add one cubit to my
stature? I'm afraid it did not. One idea, however, came to
me on shipboard going home. It was a most unlikely setting
to be thinking about anything, but you can't be exposed to
the East without having some of its philosophy rub off. The
first night out of Yokohama on the S.S. *President Hoover*, I
was having a drink in the grand ballroom, the tall Corin-
thian columns of which made a bizarre contrast to the lines
of slot machines on either wall. A crummy band was playing "Body and Soul," and I was thinking about Karma.
Not to be too Russian, just what is a soul I asked myself.
One thing I knew. People who think they have one get
quite fierce on the subject, but when pinned down they go
all esoteric and fuzzy. Everyone agrees that the soul is not
a person's brains or personality. It is something yet again—
one's conscience, emotions, id, the ultimate gift one can

give another, the dweller within, maybe even a stray bit of cosmos broken off from the whole. Whatever it is, this ineffable something is thought to be immortal. I didn't want to knock the concept—Karma was better than the recycling of life bit; nobody really wants to turn up again as a cactus —but I couldn't accept the idea that the soul was so impersonal, so pure, so stripped of all idiosyncrasies and foibles. Who said these things are unfit for immortality? They are so much a part of us, in fact the most recognizable part, it seemed to me that it ducked the issue completely to commit them to oblivion. Such a dehumanized soul was no longer you or I, just a stodgy little residue, immortal perhaps, but only fit for "dullsville."

Sitting across the dance floor with her mother was a girl who had exchanged smiles with me on deck. I was sure her soul was neither stodgy nor impersonal. I strongly suspected instead that it was looking forward to a fling (they don't get many in heaven). Its present earthly abode was a touch on the plump side, but compelling. She was wearing a low-cut, green silk dress and a jade pendant which stood out against her remarkably white skin. It could have been that we were destined.

CHAPTER

Upon my return to New York City, Father and I had a little talk, the burden of which was that since my formal education was over, it was time now for me to buckle down and go to work. I've never been very keen on work, but the validity of his position was unarguable, given the current mores. It's a curious thing, but up until the last century nobody in his right mind would go to an office eight hours a day, five days a week unless he absolutely had to. Today all that has changed. There seems to be a renaissance in our culture, not of arts and letters, but of condottiere types out for money and power. Even people with plenty of money are starting at the bottom, and quite a few are making it to the top. They do it, they say, to prove themselves, but surely there is little that is commendable in the process. Climbing over the less determined is as easy as rolling off a log for the ambitious and able.

The trouble is that these values are implanted in us by the Protestant work ethic, which is still too much in evidence. It's wrong not to work, and work hard; one must be a "keen competitor"; "man's reach should exceed his grasp." Prodded by these ferocious yardsticks, the life of the average fellow becomes well-nigh intolerable. When you get right down to it, it's all those people with inferior grasps that fill the sanatoriums.

I thought it best not to go into all this with Father who had started work at the bottom as a "runner" on Wall Street. A runner in those days was the term applied to messenger boys who effected the actual exchange of stock certificates. Father said he knew the first day that Wall Street was where he wanted to be. The air was electric, he said, and he loved it. My own reaction to the world of high finance was a little less clear-cut. Father had arranged to have me absorbed into the research department of Dominick and Dominick, where I was assigned a desk and given a book to read about "The Street."

All books on complicated subjects are the same in that the opening paragraphs are deceptively simple. In the case of the Wall Street book, it started off gently enough with a group of merchants sitting around under a butternut tree exchanging their wares—all very cozy and easy to understand. But in Chapter Two it plunged into the subject of wheat futures—i.e., selling stuff that not only wasn't there, but didn't even exist. I decided then that such mind as I had was not meant for this kind of thing. You have to be interested in money *per se* to really enjoy the Street.

Manipulating money for the pure joy of making more money is an all-consuming passion for two types of people —those who want to be very rich, and those who are. The trouble is the former will never catch up with the latter. The awesome gap between the rich and the very rich has been growing wider for years.

There was a time when to be a simple millionaire was something, especially the English variety, when a millionaire in the days of the five-dollar pound was automatically five times richer than his American counterpart. Today in the United States, however, in order to get in this league you have to be a multimillionaire. I should say twenty-five million would be about rock bottom. Although Americans don't really approve of people with money, there seems to be a worship of the very rich ingrained in the national character. Every summer in Newport, thousands of tourists troop through the great houses on Bellevue Avenue obviously enjoying the grandeur. They even glow with national pride when the guide at "The Breakers" assures them that the ceiling in the great hall is just as ornate as any ceiling in Europe. Even among the very rich themselves, the richest man at dinner sits on the right of the hostess and the second richest on her left. The protocol was established years ago at a Newport dinner to which both the ex-President of the United States and J. P. Morgan were invited. The seating was never in doubt.

A certain amount of money is essential to lead a favored life, but as my great-aunt Carrie said to her niece, "Money don't bring happiness, Janie." The keynote to its enjoyment is to keep one's tastes relatively simple. Since only multimillionaires can match the materialistic splendor of the nineteenth-century milords, one might just as well forget it. Obviously I would prefer to ride ten miles in a straight line over my land to get to the sea, but this being difficult on the Connecticut shore, I have settled for something less. We all have our crosses to bear.

Enormous wealth today seems anachronistic. My Republican friends consider me a "parlor pink" because I don't believe in laissez-faire capitalism. Furthermore, I don't think that *The New York Times* is Communist-inspired. And in addition, I have always voted Democratic. All this distresses them. "But you are a beneficiary of capitalism," they say. "You enjoy the good life." I do. The fact that I look and act very much like them is even more distressing, but I believe what J.F.K. once said, "Those who make peaceful revolution impossible, make violent revolution inevitable." In that I prefer the former type of revolution to the latter, I consider myself a conservative. We now have world inflation, recession, depression. People blame it on the Arabs, the Commies, the unions, the U.N., the welfare state, almost anything will do as the villain of the piece except the consumption principle on which the country has prospered. Mass production has worked miracles, but unfortunately we have instilled in everyone the idea that they should want more and more, even though the output is finite. We can't go back to the days when clouds of little Irish maids provided service for a pittance. Today their grandchildren would never dream of working so hard for so little. And who would blame them?

In the land of rising expectations, the adman is king. Uneasy lies his head, however, in times of mass unemployment. Take the TV commercial for Chrysler that must have made every ghetto bar in the country. A sexy girl's voice murmurs enticingly "Your next car" and there, slowly revolving in front of one's eyes, is a gleaming Chrysler Imperial. "Your next car" she says again and the background music swells. This I submit is unhealthy. For every home with a possible buyer of this Imperial, there must be five thousand viewers for whom there is never going to be a next car, or if there is, it will be a beaten up old jalopy. The prevalence of looting during ghetto riots is small wonder to me. The wonder is they didn't blow up the Imperials. TV advertising that caters to the few without a thought for the many who are watching, can get us all in trouble. This is not to say that I am a *status quo* man at heart, just a word of advice to those who are. It has always seemed to me that if the United States is to survive as a world power, its future role must adhere more to the principles of its revolutionary past than the practices of its bourgeois present.

When I was at Yale I had two roommates, one of whom read Karl Marx and the other *Burke's Peerage*. At the risk of sounding as though the former had won me over, there is something shocking to me in the picture of a man soaking up the sun on a beach while his holdings on the Street make more in a day than fifty percent of the American population make in a year. I know the arguments for it—his money is giving work to others, it is venture capital that made this country great, he has risked his money and may lose it—but at the same time there's always the argument in rebuttal of some miner chipping away at the end of a dark tunnel for chicken feed. I am a beneficiary of capitalism, but I tend to agree with Chairman Mao that "the socialist system will eventually replace the capitalist system" and that "this is an objective law independent of man's will." The alternative, of course, is for IBM to split twenty for one, and as a patriotic gesture give one share each to all the underprivileged. This might make for some confusion amongst the Hottentots, Masai and others, but it would take care of well over two billion people in the sense that they would have a share in American capitalism and ipso facto would resist the blandishments of Moscow.

As I have intimated, however, I have no head for this sort of thing and soon left Wall Street for the more congenial atmosphere of Time Inc. At least I thought *Time* was going to be more congenial. I had joined their "college boy/office boy squad" and should have known by the terminology that no good was ever going to come of it. About six or seven of us were jammed into a little slit of an office with a bench, a table and a pigeonhole contrivance for mail. There was also a buzzer which summoned whoever happened to be sitting on the outside end of the bench. It worked on the same principle as a taxi line. Answering the buzzer could mean anything from delivering a cup of coffee to lugging some advertising plates back to their originating agency.

I drew a little horror once which consisted of carrying twenty copies of *Fortune* to a Mr. Li at Columbia University. Unfamiliar with the Westside subway, I took the express into the depths of Harlem where I emerged with my twenty copies at the bottom of Morningside Heights. The stairway to the top is graceful, but there must be five hundred steps which when multiplied by twenty copies of a heavy magazine like *Fortune* makes for absolute zero in pleasure.

In addition to the buzzer work, we had regular routine assignments on a weekly basis, such as staying late and seeing that all the windows were closed (no air conditioning!) or putting soap and paper towels in the lavatories. The latter chore had its moments. Although the supply of soap and towels was meant to be refurbished while the lavatories were unoccupied, I somehow always ran a little late and found myself in the women's lavatory as the ladies were arriving. No cheap thrills to be sure, but as a student of the opposite sex, it was interesting to record their reactions to a man in their inner sanctum. Married women and the types who had lived went right about their business with a cheery greeting; the unattractive recoiled and would wait outside until I emerged.

Unfortunately, in everything there is a right way of doing things and an easy way. I am peculiarly gifted in sniffing out the easy way. Applied to the Time Inc. mail room, this took the form of spending more and more time away on errands before returning to the taxi line on the bench. Needless to say I didn't exactly forge up through the ranks. In fact as the summer wore on into fall and winter I could see myself becoming a permanent fixture in the mail room, with the only hope of getting out of it either being fired or an early retirement at fifty. I have never been ambitious, but this eventuality began to haunt me. I could even see my obituary. "Mr. Barnard joined Time Inc., where after twenty-five years he rose to be Number 2 in their mail room."

At about this time I met at a cocktail party the head of

the Crowell Publishing Co. that put out *Collier's* magazine amongst other things. Mr. Crowell was one of those gray-haired, granite-faced tycoons who had obviously conquered everything in sight. To my surprise he listened with apparent interest when I told him I wanted to write. *Collier's* was then featuring a one-page short story in each issue, and the next day at his suggestion I sent him my latest. I sensed it was not quite right for his publication, but it was short. The title was *The Man who Shat at Will.* Psychiatrists weave their theories about dreams, but to me dreams are based simply on one's physical condition at the time of dreaming. My story is a case in point. I had just taken some milk of magnesia and dreamed of a little man with a Stan Laurel expression who went about New York in a bowler hat and a short Brooks Brothers raincoat crapping whenever he felt like it. After performing, say, in front of a picture at the Museum of Modern Art, he would move on and there it would be on the floor. Nobody ever suspected him because of his costume, he was even wearing striped trousers under his raincoat. What they didn't know was that he was wearing no underwear and that the elegant trousers gracing his shoes ended just above the knees where they were held in place by elongated suspenders. Mr. Crowell liked the idea but said it was not for *Collier's.*

I didn't leave *Time* right away. Nevertheless, on the strength of this faint encouragement I embarked on a literary career. While commuting from Long Island, I took up reading Aldous Huxley's *Point Counter Point* to improve my vocabulary. If you read Huxley carefully—i.e., don't skip and look up every word you don't understand—it's a liberal education in itself—for example, words like "crapulous" (hung over) and "steatopygous" (fat-assed) and the phrase "piling Pelion on Ossa." (Zeus gave the Titans the task of putting Mt. Pelion on top of Mt. Ossa.) Not too useful but erudite. I also enrolled in a series of night courses at Columbia: short-story writing, playwriting, and, to add profundity, a few ancillary subjects such as "Comparative Religion" and "World Perspectives in Modern Literature." The latter was conducted by a bright young man with a shaved head like Yul Brynner. To compensate, he wore black-framed spectacles and black shirts with a red or yellow tie. The net effect was that of sitting in a Communist cell and being harangued by a Commissar. We read *War and Peace, The Magic Mountain, Moby Dick, Emperor and Gallilean* and others—each had a whopping big theme. The effect on my short-story writing was definitive. I stopped. You can't cram much "weltschmerz" into a Cosmopolitan formula.

The need for scope in my writing led me down a bizarre literary bypath of my own invention—a movie script with all the camera directions in haiku-type blank verse in the style of the T'ang poets, or at least what I took to be such verse. The opening scene gives the form:

As the camera *pans*
Over the Appenines
We *fade*
To a *close-up* of
Lars Porsena
Eating grapes.

The title of this opus was *The False Etruscan*, the one who lingered in his home when Lars Porsena of Clusium was on the march for Rome. I always sympathized with the false Etruscan as one who was only doing what came naturally. Instead of the shame that Macaulay would have heaped upon his head, I had him marching from success to success in the boudoirs of Clusium while his compatriots were slogging through the Pontine marshes.

The theme, of course, was antiwar, which was as popular then as it is today. But aside from the wooden love scenes and the long pacifist diatribes, the cost of production

would have completely ruined any studio. In the final
scene a cast of thousands lined the Tiber—on both sides.
Masses of triremes plied the Mediterranean and, as I remember, the script called for:

> A *wide-angle shot*
> Of their total
> Destruction
> By fire.

Cecil B. DeMille, to whom I sent the script, replied that
his production schedule was already full. Alexander Korda
and J. Arthur Rank didn't answer. The Library of Congress
sent me a receipt for the remaining two typewritten copies.
To get through life easily, I recommend strongly against attempting to be a genius.

There was a girl in my "World Perspectives" course who
always sat in the front row, while I normally sat in the rear.
As the course progressed I had ample opportunity to admire her long blonde hair curled under in a pageboy. Un-
like some girls who look very well from behind and turn out
to have the face of a horse, she had a pretty, upturned face
with bright blue, innocent eyes and a very ladylike expression. We had a beer together on Amsterdam Avenue after
the last class in the spring and discussed James Joyce's
Ulysses. I could tell as we drank our beer that she was certainly a virgin and very innocent. We made a date for dinner the following week in Beekman Place where she lived
with another girl on the top floor of a walk-up.

On the appointed evening, a warm one, I was definitely
out of sorts after trudging up four flights to find no one
home. There was an Italian restaurant next door, and I
popped in to nurse my injured pride only to find her seated
at the first table having coffee with another girl and a man.
Covered with confusion at having forgotten, she insisted
that I come back to the apartment and she would make
good on her offer of a meal. I remember looking wistfully at

a heaping plate of spaghetti at the next table, but accepted, and back we trudged up the stairs.

The other couple, who were engaged, went to bed immediately leaving us full use of the living room. The latter, a high-ceilinged studio, was sparsely furnished—a cushion-covered day bed with a coffee table in front of it seemed the only place to sit, except for some high stools by a bar in the corner. The kitchen consisted of a small closet opening off the main room and my friend, Terry, after mixing a Martini for me and pouring a brandy for herself, disappeared therein with the door open.

"How do you like my Hegelian triad?" she asked from inside.

"Your what?"

"The painting."

"Oh, yes," I said. I had missed the lecture on Hegel.

On an easel in front of a tall window was a canvas with the design of a left and right profile of a woman's head, which when looked at for a moment revealed that it was actually a full face in the manner of Picasso. I could see I was in for an intellectual evening—just one of those things to put up with—probably complete with a long discussion of *Les Fauves.*

Terry, however, was an excellent cook. A delicious egg dish was followed by a brandy and coffee and I began to feel that I could talk about *Les Fauves* for quite some time. We were sitting together on the day bed.

"I couldn't be more apologetic," she said. "It just went out of my head completely."

"You rallied beautifully."

"No, no. So rude. How can I make it up to you? More brandy?" she asked brightening. She got up with a catlike grace I hadn't been conscious of before.

"You move well," I said.

"Thank you, sir. I should. Two years with Martha Graham."

She came back from the bar and I noticed that her blouse had become unbuttoned, just the top two buttons, but enough to reveal the start of her firm, high bosom.

"You have many talents," I said.

She had rejoined me on the couch and was lying with her hands behind her head. The partially opened blouse spread open further.

"I should have put on some music. I love music," she said. "You know I was once trying to get into Carnegie Hall —it was an all-Stravinsky program, an absolute sellout—so I climbed up the fire escape and found myself in the electrician's booth. A nice man, he invited me in and we lay down on the floor together and I watched and heard the whole thing for free. Well, not exactly . . ." She smiled her innocent smile. "I tried to pay him but he wouldn't take the money."

By now one of her breasts was completely free of the blouse and I saw that the nipple was distended. I brushed it gently.. "You have a generous nature," I said and kissed her. Immediately her tongue explored my mouth and my hand progressed. My God, how the waters come down at Lahore, I thought, remembering the girl in *Ulysses*. She gave a little moan and my free hand touched her eyelids. It seemed only decent to close those big, blue, virginal eyes.

I saw quite a bit of Terry that spring. As Catherine the Great said, "Nothing in my opinion is more difficult to resist than what gives one pleasure—all arguments to the contrary are prudery." We were not in love in the sense of wanting to say "I love you" over and over again—we never mentioned the subject—but we did have fun and games.

One of them took us to Allentown, Pennsylvania—a place I had never been to before (or since). It was quite a one-night stand. A cousin of mine who was being sent to a drying-out ranch somewhere in the West had joined us for lunch in New York and pleaded with us to drive with him that afternoon, just to get him started on his way. An im-

pulsive girl, Terry agreed, thinking it would be only kind—
he did seem a little shaky—so off we went in my cousin's
car into the wilds of New Jersey. After about two hours
driving (there were no big thruways then) we all agreed we
needed a drink, but New Jersey was having some kind of
an election that day so all the bars were shut. By then we
had gotten to a small town called Anthony which had
seemed a good place to stop since it reminded my cousin
and me of our old drinking bouts at Anthony's on Long
Island. A cop told us we would have to go to Pennsylvania.
Allentown, he said, would be better than Bethlehem.

As we drove into Allentown, night was falling and it was
obvious we were going to need lodging of some sort. Fortunately the place seemed to be full of rather sleazy-look-
ing hotels, so we chose the best of the lot and booked two
rooms, one for Terry and me and an adjoining one for my
cousin.

Cousin Lawrence—he was also descended from the fellow
who had climbed the ramparts at Acre—may have had a
problem with drink, but he had a healthy, normal appetite
when it came to women. After several false starts with the
waitress in the dining room, he accepted her suggestion
that she call a friend who sometimes went out with travel-
ing salesmen. I could see the descendant of Acre wince at
being placed in this category, but under the circumstances
(he was well in his cups), it was the best that could be
done. Terry and I retired to our room and listened to him
pacing around on the other side of the door.

We didn't have to wait. The buzzer rang next door
and we could hear indistinctly a murmur of conversation.

"I hope she's nice," said Terry. "Your cousin is sweet."

We lay in the half-light listening. Suddenly there was
another buzz on the door and another voice and the sound
of a table being wheeled in and the rattle of dishes.

"She must be hungry," I said.

"I am too," said Terry. "Kiss me, Hardy." She smiled.

It was in the aftermath of lovemaking that there came a few tentative knocks on the door between the adjoining rooms.

"Now what?" I said getting up. Cousin Lawrence looked awful standing in the doorway. He had on only his pajama bottoms, his hair was tousled and his eyes were slits.

"The bitch," he said. "She's gone."

"What?"

"Yes. Ate a full course meal—soup, steak and potatoes, apple pie a la mode—and then packed off."

"You've been had all right," I said. "Have a seat."

Lawrence sat down on the bed which wasn't exactly what I had in mind.

"Poor boy," said Terry. "There . . . there . . ." She began to stroke the back of his neck.

Suddenly he plunged his head in his hands, shaking violently.

"I'm just no good," he sobbed.

"Put your head here," said Terry softly. "You've had a lot to drink."

Lawrence snuggled in and Terry had her arm around him, patting him gently. I sat down in an overstuffed chair and began to flip through the pages of the Gideon Bible.

"This kindness bit," I said, "there's no need to overdo it."

"Shsh," said Terry. "He's asleep already."

"Great," I said rather grumpily, "I'll go next door."

"We can all fit on this bed."

"Thanks," I said and slammed the door behind me.

I awoke about 5:00 A.M. Dawn was just stealing into Allentown, but it was the voices in the next room that got me. The door flew open.

"He wants to marry me," said Terry.

"Yes," said Lawrence, "We're engaged."

Now the hours between 5:00 A.M. and breakfast in Allentown are not the best time to plan a lifetime of happiness, but we tried. It was decided that Lawrence should continue on his way to the drying-out ranch to see if he was really in love, and we would get a ring with which he would plight his troth as soon as the shops opened at 9:00 A.M. The ring idea was mine. It was really sort of a sop because he wanted Terry to continue the drive out West and I could see she was reluctant, but didn't know how to say no without hurting his feelings. We got a ring at 9:15, a miserable little diamond, the kind you used to see advertised along with a pony, both of which would be yours if you sold so many packets of bluing, but all parties to the transaction were delighted—the man who sold it, Lawrence because it represented something tangible in his disordered life, and Terry because she was kind.

We drove with Lawrence as far as a gas station outside of Allentown proper, and after what seemed to me a rather long embrace, even for those so recently engaged, we waved him a final goodbye.

"He's so sweet," said Terry.

"You're not going to marry him, are you?"

"Oh, no. But that ring was a nice idea. I think it made him happy. Did you notice when he put it on my finger?"

"Shaking like a leaf," I said.

"No, his expression," she said. "Very gentle and lost."

A trailer truck pulled in for gas and we got a ride back to New York, Terry and the driver chatting cozily about his wife and kids.

Needless to say with a girl like Terry in the offing, my literary labors faltered. I can never understand how certain people achieve the dual fame of being great swordsmen and at the same time producers of great art. After lovemaking I'm right back in that old "Who cares what banks fail in Yonkers?" syndrome. And yet if we are to believe the legends, some people climb out of bed, rush to the typewriter, piano, or easel and whip off a masterpiece apparently inspired by Eros.

Unfortunately this type of thing seems to be what separates the men from the boys. Good sexual relations turn the average fellow into a zombie, incapable of doing much more than crossing the street without getting run over. One used to hear much about religion being the opiate of the people, but the real opiate, of course, is sex. Given good sex, serfs, washroom attendants, and riveters tend to view the status quo through rose-colored glasses. Once this takes place the powers that be are even more firmly in the drivers seat, whether they be corporate managers or chiefs of state. Strangely enough the only government to grasp this fact and capitalize on it is in Sweden where, I'm told, the Social Democrats kept the populace dazed and malleable for the past forty-four years by disseminating information on erotic techniques.

I didn't stop writing all at once; I found that the formats used were simply getting shorter and shorter. I wrote a play about this time, primarily because one could fill up space so easily writing for the stage. For example, a good half-page can be knocked off as follows:

MRS. PONSONBY-JONES: *Yes?*
SIR HENRY FLUTEFALL: *No!*
MRS. PONSONBY-JONES: *Indeed?*
SIR HENRY FLUTEFALL: *Never.*
MRS. PONSONBY-JONES: *Never?*
SIR HENRY FLUTEFALL: *Never!*

With competent actors and a good director, I've always felt this little passage could be extremely effective theatre.

My pursuit of the dramatic arts led me into a strange byway, namely, Orwigsburg, Pennsylvania, where I had a nonpaying job with a summer stock company as a play doctor. This consisted of cutting the play to fit the cast and writing in lines to smooth over the excisions, not exactly *Hamlet* without Hamlet, but that idea. I remember sitting up all one night rewriting *Idiot's Delight* because the man who played Alfred Lunt's part got drunk and smashed himself up in a car two nights before we opened. I like to think he wasn't missed.

Approaching Orwigsburg by car, you drive through the towns of Bird-in-Hand, Rising Sun, Intercourse, and Blue Ball—in that order, which gives some people pause—but soon you are in rolling farm country settled by the Amish almost three hundred years ago. The big trucks roar on the ribbon of roads bisecting the fertile fields and you are in the heart of rural America with all the presumed virtues that the phrase implies. The Amish, or Mennonites, came over to America from Holland and Switzerland at the end of the seventeenth century to practice their own brand of religious belief. The solemn, bearded men in high-crowned hats and their women in poke bonnets, all in black and sitting bolt upright in their horse-drawn buggies, were a strange contrast to our group of would-be Thespians from the Columbia Drama School. I felt there must be a story here somewhere. There was, but it had nothing to do with the Amish.

Our troupe, which included a few broken-down professionals, was housed in various lodgings within walking distance of the boardinghouse where we ate. The heart and soul of the latter was a wiry little woman who not only cooked the meals and washed up, but made the beds, ordered the food, mowed the lawn, and weeded an extensive garden of tomatoes. Her husband, a corpulent lout, lay in a hammock all day drinking beer and eyeing the harelipped serving girl, who also did a lot of resting outside. I don't know what kind of trees there were around the boardinghouse, but you could feel the desire under them. Presently the inevitable happened. One night when we were all in the theater doing our make-believe, the drunken husband ran off with the girl and the hardworking wife collapsed in the kitchen where she was found dead in the morning. It topped our trumped-up drama on the boards.

Here in real life was a ready-made plot, but my ability to use it was curtailed by my ignorance of the characters as people. I couldn't flesh them out. You have to write about what you know. I made some notes on the purity of the countryside and thought of the time I had gone to Vermont with visions of thick rich cream on porridge, only to find that the thick rich cream had been shipped to New York and all we got was skimmed milk. Sometimes one expects too much of rural America. The big city never looked so clean and clear on my return—it was one of those rare days with the skyline sharply etched on blue.

That winter I balanced my literary efforts in New York with a good deal of intensive skiing. Enthusiasm for the sport, which had burgeoned the year before, grew to a mania. The "Subway Alumni," as they were sometimes called, took to the slopes en masse. Ski-trains leaving Grand Central Station at 7:00 A.M. would take them to the Berkshires and then return home that night. It was a full day—breakfast in the dining car on the way up, skiing until 4:00 P.M., then sandwiches, song and glue-wine on the way back. Not quite Arlberg, but all very old world.

Presiding over these excursions in a vague advisory capacity was my Uncle Jay, who looked like a displaced member of the Austrian royal family. Jay was Mother's brother who had never worked in his life and had gone through two reasonable fortunes buying numerous cars, a biplane, and such oddments as a husky called Lobo that was one of the team that carried serum to Nome, Alaska. The most flattering thing that Father ever said to me was

Uncle Jay as displaced Austrian Grand Duke

that I had more brains in my little finger than Jay had in his head. Jay had something, however—style maybe. For one thing he had a knack of making you feel you were engaged in a most important and hazardous venture no matter what you were doing, even if it was just walking down Madison Avenue to buy ski wax. I don't ever recall seeing him actually ski, and the only advice I ever heard him give on the train was to tell someone that the dining car was forward. I should have made more of a study of Jay. He was a splendid character. Years later he met an untimely end—shot by an outraged husband while having a tryst in Schrafft's. I could have fleshed *him* out. He also collected stamps.

The last resort of a writer putting off writing is research. Terry, who as I say was always in the offing, suggested the following spring that a little back-to-the-soil movement would be beneficial to my career. She put it gently, but I rather sensed at the time that this was to be some sort of matrimonial test. We picked Jones Beach as a likely site and spent the first night with my family on Long Island getting ready for the enterprise. Fortunately, Mother and Father were out for dinner as I had grave doubts as to their warming to Terry. I was quite right, considering what occurred the following day at breakfast.

Father was reading the *Wall Street Journal* and finishing his coffee when Terry, in a low-cut diaphanous outfit of her own creation, drifted into the dining room. After introductions Terry opened up her big blue eyes on Father and explained that she had felt the call of the sea so she had been wandering down the lane.

"Harumph," said Father, getting up and folding his paper. "I hope you found it."

"Oh yes," said Terry. "It was wonderful in the early morning light. The mist . . ." Her voice trailed off since Father had already left the room.

Later as I popped my head into his study to say goodbye, he didn't even look up from his book. "Son," he said, "you have got yourself a hot potato." It was a curiously old-fashioned verdict, but you might say he had hit the nail on the head.

Jones Beach in those days was not as crowded as today, but you still had to drive considerably beyond the main complex to get away from it all. We chose a deserted stretch of the Ocean Parkway by the bird sanctuary and, with the natural secretiveness of youth, parked the car under the road in a shallow culvert.

The first order of business, of course, was to build a shelter—the old nesting instinct—and a fire—very atavistic—to keep off the saber-toothed tigers. I had brought along two rubber ponchos, mosquito netting, a blanket, and a ball of string for emergencies—not nearly enough for comfortable living on the dunes as it turned out. Terry insisted that we had to lie on something as well as having something over us. Her insistence made me wonder if perhaps we were drifting apart. We worked in silence for a while, collecting wood. I had in mind a structure lashed together with the string and the ponchos forming a roof, but after several attempts in which all the component parts sagged into the middle, Terry withdrew from the project.

"I should have known," she said.

"What?" I snapped.

When urban man attempts to pit himself against nature, his inability to cope tends to make him testy. A friend of mine described the mood as "having a dead baby." I was definitely having a dead baby as we started the evening meal—a simple repast of hot dogs toasted on sticks and a little Bourbon whiskey—but with the intake of the latter I began to mellow. Retrieving my frankfurter from the fire where it had fallen, due to a poor choice of stick, I even waxed quite eloquent on the gourmet effect of ashes. They were certainly better than sand, the fate of my second endeavor.

Quietly we watched the fire go out, thinking of God and Nietzsche, and then settled down in a ball with one poncho underneath our upper halves and the other on top, together with the blanket and mosquito netting. The trouble with this kind of thing is that in order to get away from the whine of the mosquitoes you have to bury your head inside the blanket, but then you can't breathe. No air. Never have I had such a night—hot, damp, and drafty on the edges for the one in the back spoon position. Even my hand cupped on Terry's bosom failed to bring any solace.

Morning came early as it does to most campers, the sun low on the beach and very astronomical. The ocean changed from a wine-dark sea to something more Robinson Crusoe-like. The sandpipers skittered and we had a skinny dip while the coffee was brewing.

"Thoreau had something," I said, putting the night out of mind.

"He had a roof over his head," said Terry.

This seemed a jarring note, but I let it pass. Women when they get in moods hold them longer than men. Probably something to do with the moon. Nonetheless, she looked terrific. Terry was one of those girls who plunge seal-like in the sea letting their hair go sleek and long. Normally, I'm a pushover for this approach, connoting as it does a oneness with nature and the back of the hand to Elizabeth Arden. This particular morning, however, I wanted to absent myself from felicity a while and work on another project I had formulated during the night.

We had brought along some beer which was absolutely essential for a lunch of ham and cheese on rye, but the beer was lukewarm. I wanted to redeem myself as a practical type by constructing a beer cooler out of materials at hand on the beach. The morning passed in gratifying manual labor. My idea was to harness nature to the task, something short of the Grand Coulee Dam, but in essence the same principle of making nature work for man. Beneath the shallow water the sand was much cooler; the beer bottles, therefore, should be buried in this cool packing with some sort of device to mark their whereabouts. I submerged six bottles in the wet sand with a string tied around their individual necks, the other end of each string tied to a clam shell. The strings with the shells dangling were then looped over a crossbar supported by a forked branch. The end result was quite decorative. I lay there like Hemingway's hero looking at the bridge. The shells clicked against each other occasionally in the light breeze that had come up and I dozed.

Terry woke me.

"I hate to tell you, but . . ."

The tide had risen considerably during my snooze and there was not a trace showing of my morning's endeavor. I rushed out in the water to see if anything had survived. Nothing.

"And the wind shall say," said Terry, "Here were decent, godless people, their only monument the asphalt road and a thousand lost golf balls."

"Very apt," I said, but the dead baby had returned. Cumulative failure hardens a man, dims his finer perceptions. That afternoon we explored the bird sanctuary on the other side of the road—reeds inshore and shallow sand flats stretching out in the bay. A vast colony of seagulls rose like a torn umbrella, each gull vigorously protesting our approach. Anchored just off the shallows was an old cabin-cruiser. Its occupant, a senior citizen in brown cotton shorts and a dirty yachting cap, had anchored his dinghy on the flat and was wading with a pail looking intently at the bottom.

Terry with her instinct for human contact hailed him. The senior citizen straightened up and grinned. He was a big man with the hairs on his chest bristling over his undershirt.

"Say," he said, "I've been wasting my time squinting after mussels. What can I do for you?"

The upshot was, as it always was with Terry, we joined him for dinner on his craft. As we came aboard that evening, we were greeted cheerily by an overblown blonde emerging from the cabin with an apron over her blue jeans. "Hi," she said, "I'm Maggie—Harry's girl friend." It seems that the two were fugitives from the cloak and suit business in New York, but that just placed them geographically. The outstanding fact about them was that they were unabashedly in love.

"Maggie and I have been coming here for years," said Harry. He had removed his yachting cap for dinner, revealing a shiny pate, and was wearing a turtleneck sweater. We were sitting on camp chairs in the stern, drinking whiskey.

"Nothing like it," said Maggie. "One month here makes the rest of the year worthwhile."

"How do you manage it with your respective mates?" I asked. It had come out over the whiskey that they were both married, but not to each other.

"Oh," said Maggie. "Simple. Harry's wife hates anything to do with the sea, particularly boats, and I tell Morris—that's my husband—that I'm going to the mountains to see my sister."

"This is our tenth year," said Harry. He reached over and patted Maggie's hand.

"I'd like to fall in love," said Terry.

I started to say something but Harry had the floor.

"A man can have ten mistresses if he flirts with his wife in public. Remember that young fella."

"Yes, but you've got something special," I said.

"You can say that again." He beamed at Maggie with pride. "She was a hat-check girl, you know."

"Harry!" said Maggie. "Don't mention my wicked past."

Terry had gotten up and was leaning over the rail looking at the stars.

"You're very lucky," she said.

"It's a funny thing," said Maggie, "but the only time you are truly alive is when you're in love."

"No doubt of that," said Harry.

I looked at the two of them looking at each other. Harry with his bald head and sweater actually resembled an old turtle and Maggie certainly had seen better days, but by Maggie's own definition they both were truly alive. It was all there in their eyes.

We slept on board that night, up under the bow in a sort of cocoon made out of moth-eaten cushions and shawls. It was a bit stuffy despite the air vent over our heads, but dry and a great improvement on the beach.

"That, my dear, is the goal," I whispered.

"It's the only supernatural I believe in," said Terry.

In the main cabin Harry was snoring gently. It was a rhythmic sound and, together with the lapping of the water against the hull, it made a peaceful ambience in which to contemplate the future.

CHAPTER

Although my mistress' eyebrow was pleasing, I began to feel it was high time to progress from the third to the fourth stage in Shakespeare's ages of man. I should be seeking "the bubble reputation even in the cannon's mouth" and all I was doing was "sighing like a furnace" in bed. This happens to lazy men with a modicum of talent and enough money not to starve if they sit on their duffs and do nothing. It could have been worse. Obviously, here were all the makings of a drunk, a queer, or both. The fact that I didn't turn into either, I attribute more to Karma than any resolve of mine. The thought of a drink the morning after makes me want to retch. Also, when inflamed, my wants are distressingly normal. Nevertheless I was immobilized. There were so many things to think about.

A presidential campaign was in full swing in the fall of 1936. To my mind, Thoreau summed up politics by saying that for anyone who "endeavors to contemplate the true state of things, the political state can hardly be said to have any existence whatever." Earl Browder of the American Communist Party probably got as close as anyone could to the true state of things in his condemnation of the United States political scene. According to Browder, you list on one side of the ledger all the Democrats from arch-conservative down through liberal-radical and on the other side a similar list of all the Republicans from arch-conservative to liberal-radical. Every four years there's a big hoopla and furor. Sometimes one lot gets in and sometimes the other, but it doesn't really make any difference because the two lists are roughly equivalent, with a few more liberals on the Democrat side. What Mr. Browder wanted to do was to take the two lists and draw a line horizontally between them with all the conservative Republicans and Democrats on one side and all the liberal-radicals of both parties on the other. Strangely enough, Mr. William Rusher of the ultra-conservative *National Review* recently advocated the same approach. Mr. Browder said we would have blood in the streets, which may be going too far for Mr. Rusher, but from both their points of view the horizontal line versus the present vertical arrangement makes sense. Personally, I prefer the vertical, but I never can understand how grown men can get very excited about our elections. And yet they do. Father was in a white rage during the entire campaign inveighing against "that man in the White House." So were all his friends. So was Harold, the chauffeur, who was convinced that FDR had sold out the country to the Russians. Mother continued to suggest impeachment, but never wavered in her support of Eleanor.

I wandered back into this hotbed of reactionaries with my head full of Omar Khayyám, not only the jug of wine bit, but the big one used by Gauguin—"Into this universe and why not knowing, nor whence like water willy nilly flowing, and out of it like wind along the waste, willy nilly blowing."

Father collared me.

"Son," he said, "this is probably the most important election we have ever had. You've got to understand that."

He then proceeded to explain how I could help in the noble cause. It seems that someone on his fund-raising committee had been worrying about lining up the vote of all the maids on Park Avenue; a subcommittee had been formed with blocks of apartment houses assigned, and Father had offered my services as a doorbell ringer.

I was appalled, first of all at the thoroughness of the planning—no stone left unturned. Also I had a deep-seated feeling that the maids should be allowed to make up their own minds and that probably they were already harangued too much by their employers. And that little scene in the vestibule! What did one wear to proselytize someone's cook, a cutaway and a white carnation? I must have looked shifty and evasive because Father didn't press me, a remarkable trait in a man of his convictions.

"Don't tell them you will, if you won't," he said.

"I won't," I replied, which was just cryptic enough to keep everybody happy.

The maid-employer relationship in all those nooks and crannies in the granite facade of Park Avenue struck my fancy more than how they were all going to vote. As a result I wrote a poem, at least I thought it was a poem, about one of them. I must admit that in attempting to write poetry I've never been able to free myself from the bugaboo of meter laboriously learned at school.

> The iamb saunters through my book,
> Trochees rush and tumble,
> While the anapest runs like a hurrying brook etc.

Apparently this type of thing has very little bearing in poesy today, nor did it seem to have any at the time of writing. After a brief outing in various editorial offices, the poem joined an ever increasing file of rejected literary efforts in the bottom drawer of my desk.

The election came and went and the end of the world didn't come. On Sunday mornings in New York, Father and Mother still walked down Park Avenue to St. Bartholomew's, Father with cane, top hat, and morning coat underneath his mink-lined chesterfield. The latter was a magnificent garment with an opulent collar—the kind of coat worn by Mr. Peebles, a cartoon character of the time who made a brief appearance in our national magazines. I occasionally joined them similarly attired, except for the mink-lined chesterfield. My cane, however, which I had bought in Paris, was a sword cane. Unfortunately, I had demonstrated the clever locking mechanism so much that it had a tendency to come apart, which it did one morning, leaving me with a three-foot stiletto in my hand as Father was introducing me to the president of something or other. From then on I had to use a more conventional model from his own large collection. One might think our costumes were out of style, but strangely enough we were not unique. I can't say that the majority of strollers wore top hats, but about every other block you would see two or three. It was all very ceremonial—much bowing and tipping of hats to friends and acquaintances—really quite small town and cozy. After all I used to roller skate the same route as a child.

New York, then, was still a dressy city. Monday and Friday nights at the old Metropolitan saw almost all the male occupants of the orchestra seats in white tie, as, of course, were all the men in the first tier of boxes. Also, glory of glories, the members of the Opera Club who had a large box on the second tier would exercise a privilege during the intermissions by wearing their top hats in the Louis Sherry bar. I loved it, particularly when it was snowing outside and the limousines lined up after the performance to drive people home. The best cars had cabriolet-type lanterns on the side and a wicker overlay on the doors; a few had the chauffeur bundled in fur sitting exposed to the elements with no other protection than a thin black awning over the front seat. The whole thing was very pre-revolutionary Russia and would be gone in another five years. I went to Lincoln Center recently after years of boycotting the place, but it was not the same thing at all. There's more to opera than music.

I probably would have become a member of the Opera Club if I hadn't gotten married. However, there comes a tide in the affairs of men that leads on to matrimony. At a certain age all one's contemporaries are getting married, and, like Asian flu, the contagion spreads. It is the thing to do—one must complete the social trilogy of school, college, and marriage.

A friend of mine, for whom I was an usher, was getting married in Lenox, Massachusetts, and since I knew everyone in the wedding party except one bridesmaid, I decided in a flush of romanticism that she was destined to be my wife. Her name was Diana Kissel. Fortunately for me, Diana was beautiful and funny and not a miserable drab because in the contagious euphoria of the moment I might have settled for the latter. She liked my cashmere coat; I loved her gaiety and underlying elegance, and after a long conversation at the Stork Club one night, the gist of which was that we wouldn't get married just because everyone else was, we announced our engagement.

The wedding was an absolute smash, although at first I was worried as I seemed to be the only thing my two sets of ushers had in common. Five were Yale friends; the other five, who came from the New York-Long Island area, were "insular" in the extreme. The Yale group called me Larry, whereas the Long Islanders all knew me as "Gus," for the following reason: Father, whose name was Augustus, had a reputation for ferocity, and in my early youth my childhood friends had started calling me Gus behind his back. One of them once called up the house and asked for Gus, and Mother summoned my father to the telephone. When Father discovered the call was for me instead of him, he slammed down the receiver, but not before barking into it,

"You wish to speak to my son? His name is *Lawrence*." My poor friend was undaunted. From that point on, the name Gus was mine for life on Long Island and has since taken over completely except for one holdout—a roommate at college, John Auchincloss, who has stoutly refused to be swayed. Happily, the two groups mixed splendidly at the wedding, owing to an almost constant flow of alcohol during the festivities.

Prior to the church ceremony, my ushers and I convened at the Union Club. The wedding was at St. James' Church, around the corner. Officiating was the rector—the humane and wise Dr. Horace W. B. Donegan, who, several years later, became Bishop of New York. A man from Brooks Brothers had been engaged to tie our ascot ties, since this is something of a lost art. A dry character, he gave the impression as he went about his task that the man who takes no interest in his clothes is fit for treason, stratagems, and spoils. His talent, of course, was highly specialized, but essential to a formal wedding. Left to our own devices, we would have been a pretty disheveled lot in the church. As the others had gone on ahead, the man from Brooks walked over to St. James' with me and wished me luck before getting into a cab. We shook hands in the street. I remember him fondly.

As it was, everybody looked pristine. I had supplied gray spats for all, in addition to the customary tie, gloves, and carnation. One hears that clothes don't make the man, but a morning coat certainly improves the outward shell. All of this blended with Diana's bevy of attendants from Lenox and Boston as they lined up in front of the choir stalls. It was just the kind of thing my old nurse, Nunny, used to read about so avidly in the *Journal-American*. One probably shouldn't be objective at one's own wedding, but then I'm an Aquarian, and we have a tendency toward detachment.

Leaving St. James' Church

One aspect that struck me forcibly was the speed of the performance. I was barely getting adjusted to my role when, before I knew it, I was man and wife 'till death do us part. Then Mendelssohn and out. Going down the aisle, I patted Mother's gloved hand on the front pew as we passed, which made Cousin Mary Horn beside her stifle a sob. I also winked at Terry in the back row on my side of the church. She smiled back, rather loftily I felt, but then we had drifted apart. I had become quite stuffy about her ability to support herself with what I can only describe as her own coinage of the realm. On emerging from the church, Diana and I embraced on the steps, at the suggestion of the photographer from Bachrach, and a small cheer went up from the knot of passersby on Madison Avenue who had gathered because of the awning.

The reception was held by Diana's family in their apartment at 10 Gracie Square. Alexander Haas and his string orchestra, in their red coats, played gypsy music; the champagne flowed and we danced. As the FDR Drive had not yet been built, the apartment looked directly out over the East River. Diana and I slipped away to the balcony off the library and dropped our empty glasses into the water. Somehow this seemed as meaningful as all those vows in church.

"A great show, darling," I said.

She laughed. "It's a shame we have to leave."

That's one of the troubles with weddings. You get all your nearest and dearest together; you have a bang-up jolly party, and then, just when things are at their best you have to disappear.

We sailed that night for Europe. During the crossing, *inter alia*, I read *Mein Kampf*. The Germans are a mixed-up lot—all that nice *Gemütlichkeit* combined with a penchant for genocide and martial conquest. One trouble is their love of music: that happy oompah band can shift with only the wave of a baton into "Deutschland Uber Alles," and then they're off on a misty-eyed version of *Cabaret*. Another trouble is that the Germans go in for walking in a big way and, as everyone knows, it's just a hop, skip and jump from hiking to marching. I had bought a German camera, of course, on arrival, and almost all my pictures of Germany showed Germans walking—first, one artistic shot of a hiker with pack alone on a country lane, then another of ten men marching with shovels, then a hundred men with shovels, then thousands parading in Munich with Nazi banners en bloc and fascist symbols on poles like Roman legionnaires. It was the "Day of Deutsches Kunst." If I'd had any sense, I would have rushed my pictures to Washington, but then presumably they had also read *Mein Kampf*, so they should have known what was coming. The menace of a country is in direct proportion to the quantity of crew haircuts in the population. Germany was bristling with short hair.

Somehow when I think of the personality of countries, I think of Germany as distinctly middle class. I suppose this is because of the Nazi movement, which was just that. On the other hand I think of Italy as aristocratic even though Fascism was much the same thing. Maybe there are more Counts than Grafs per hectare, or maybe it's just because more exportable Italians wear expensive shoes and play backgammon with abandon.

The hotel where we stayed on the island of Brioni (then Italian) was very grand. The first night we dallied around in the bedroom until 8:30 which seemed a reasonably chic hour to dine, only to be confronted in the dining room with a few scattered tables of nursemaids and their infant charges. The *haut monde* never showed up until ten or a little thereafter. My espresso was icy cold by the time the Duke of Spoleto, the top grandee, and his entourage entered the room.

The grandness of this Grand Hotel was visible everywhere. For example, all the yachts in the harbor had funnels. I don't want to sound snippish, but I do think a non-sailing pleasure craft must have a funnel if it is to qualify as a yacht. Also one of the guests had a chimpanzee (very grand indeed) which amused itself by throwing nuts from its balcony at the tables in the cocktail patio below. The hotel also had a stable of polo ponies that it rented out whenever enough people got together to play the resident Italian team led by the Duke. The ponies apparently belonged to Louis Rothschild who was spending the summer in a German jail owing to certain religious and/or ethnic differences between himself and the Nazi government.

One day we formed a hodgepodge team of three Americans and one Englishman and, mounted on "poor Louis' " ponies, set forth to do battle with the Italians. The field, which was somewhere back of the hotel and reached by a dilapidated bus, was located on the side of a hill with one goal at a considerably higher elevation than the other and with the setting sun behind it. Added to this was the fact that the playing surface was dirt, not turf. The Italians won the choice of goals to defend and obviously took the uphill one. Despite this slight advantage however, they couldn't seem to hit the ball. Led by the noble Duke, the entire team would stream after the ball shouting the Italian equivalent of "leave it!" Everyone would take a swipe anyway and miss it, then swirl back to the fray in disgust on foaming, cavorting steeds with a beautiful display of horsemanship. It was a most unusual game. We never made a goal either. Memorable, though, and very international with shouts of "Avanti!" "Deshala!" and "Piccolo questa!" (or something like that) ringing out in the clouds of dust. And then, because of the Rothschild ponies, one felt inevitably a part of history.

Life when we returned to New York was nowhere near as

opulent. For $125 a month we had rented a small apart-
ment at 430 East 86th Street which consisted of a living
room, kitchen, bedroom, and bath. There were two good
features, however, which made us take it; one was a real
fireplace, and the other was a smashing view of the
Queensboro bridge and the midtown area over the roofs of
the tenements at the back of the building. We embarked
on decorating it with terrifying intensity.

In decorating a New York apartment, there are certain
basic principles that apply. One is that, unless you are
fabulously rich and can afford to have it all created for you
by some aesthetic stripling, you have to make do with what
you've got. In the case of most young married couples, this
consists of the wedding presents and a few parental hand-
me-downs.

Happily in our case, Diana's family were great movers.
Every two years they would take over a new apartment,
knock down walls, build in bookcases with cabinets underneath, and generally act as if they had moved in for life. At
the end of another two years the process would be repeated. Every time they moved, of course, something did not fit
in the next place, so we fell heir to some goodies. We acquired a Sheraton sideboard this way and some girondelles
which, together with a "suit" of stuffed furniture bought at
Bloomingdale's and quickly slipcovered in flowered chintz,
made quite a pleasing effect. Added to these were selected
wedding presents—an elliptical, wooden coffee table,
which was then the standard gift of maiden aunts, a silver
cigarette box from my ushers, and a few well-chosen Audu-
bon prints. Some yellowish draw curtains and our first purchase, a deep purple rug (an error) completed the picture,
except for one overstuffed chair in white cheesecloth that
we never got around to covering. This was the all-passions-
spent chair. Having fought over every square foot of terrain, each of us striving for perfection as we saw it, we

decided to call a truce and lived with it uncovered for the next two years.

Our first dinner at home took four hours to prepare. It was a fairly elaborate dish involving veal and sour cream that Diana had learned in her cooking class at Bride's School. These institutions used to teach refined young ladies who had become engaged how to become, at the same time, Cordon Bleu chefs. As most of them barely knew how to boil an egg, it was rather like Miss Muffet learning how *sauce verte* could improve her curds and whey. Nevertheless, when Diana's dish was all together, it was delicious, but by then it was more of a midnight snack than a real dinner as the portions had dwindled perceptibly during the cooking.

Diana was pregnant fairly soon. We had been using the "rhythm" or Roman Catholic form of birth control. It seemed the easiest, if not the surest method in those happy-go-lucky days before the Pill. Our firstborn arrived in Doctors Hospital, red as the proverbial beet, screaming, and covered with what I can only describe as tufts of furry brown hair. I looked at her through the glass partition darkly and decided I was too young to be a father. And certainly not rich enough. Estimating the cost of a seven pound baby, in those days (1939), it came to about two hundred dollars a pound; that's including flowers and a bauble for the mother. Today, I suppose it would be considered a bargain.

Life in New York, as a young married couple, was a curiously limited affair, not that the limitations bothered us. We scruffed along happily enough. It was nice to know that if you wanted to see, hear, or buy anything it was available somewhere in the city, but we made no use of it. People who live in New York are essentially village people. Our village was Yorkville, which in those days had no big stores or apartment houses. Buying a Christmas tree in the snow on 86th Street was like something from a Schnitzler play. I always bought our tree late on Christmas Eve, when the small shop windows looked their best with their wreaths and lighted decorations. Owing to the late purchase, the tree usually required a certain amount of branch splicing to achieve the desired effect, but as Father had always refused to pay more than $1.50 for a tree, I had early training in the art and felt it vaguely traditional. Aside from three or four couples whom we saw fairly regularly, our contacts were with the butcher, grocer, druggist, and the newspaper man in his kiosk. We went to the local movies maybe twice a month, but mostly we listened to radio programs for entertainment—Fibber McGee and Molly, also Burns and Allen. Compared to color TV, this fare might seem pretty thin, but then we didn't know any better. When we went out to a restaurant, it was usually pigs knuckle and kraut at one of the nearby beer joints. Sometimes for a real splurge we went to a Swedish place on East 57th Street where the decor was more Grand Hotel and you could get a delicious smorgasbord of hot and cold hors d'oeuvres, dessert and wine for $1.75.

The economics of living then make one's mouth water today. With the arrival of the baby we had moved to another apartment on East 81st Street just off Lexington Avenue. The new apartment didn't have much of a view, but it was on the north side of the street and had sun in the front windows. It cost $150.00 a month, and for that we got two bedrooms, each with a bath, a living room with a wood-burning fireplace, a dining room, kitchen, maid's room and bath. For $60 a month we acquired a ferocious, redheaded, temporary nurse named Annie Queenie, and for another $45 a misanthropic German girl named Agnes who cooked. The subway was still just a nickel.

I was earning nothing at the time, but insofar as it was in me, I was striving manfully to write the great American novel. I used to walk down each morning to the family's house on 71st Street where I wrote in my former bedroom from nine to five every day. I would write longhand in the morning, type it in the afternoon, and edit it on the john the following morning. Overlooking the days you spend in front of a blank page, you can grind out quite a lot with such a routine and eventually get together a body of words.

At five o'clock each day I would knock off and walk around to the Union Club to play squash. Father had given me a life membership in 1935, which meant I didn't have to pay any annual dues. I realized at the time this was a good deal, provided I lived long enough, but the comforting thing to me about life membership was that, should I fall on evil times, I could always keep going with free cheese, crackers, and cocktail sausages in the bar. One could also sleep in the library, which would certainly be better than the subway where indigents slept in that less violent era. On Christmas Day there was also a members' eggnog party on the house. Everyone wore morning coats and top hats, a tradition still practiced today despite the danger of garroting that members may face as they wend their way to the festivities.

One ancient member once routed single-handedly a group of Communist sympathizers who invaded the Club portals at the time of Khrushchev's visit to New York. Khrushchev had followed up his shoe-hammering act at the United Nations with an appearance on the balcony of the Russian Embassy just across Park Avenue. The rowdies entered the front hall which gives onto a double flight of stairs down which the ancient member was slowly descending with his cane. In answer to their shouted queries as to what kind of a place they were in, unruffled, the A.M. told them in tones of cultured grace that it was a home for incurables. The group instantly fled.

At about this time I read a book that should be required

reading for any would-be writer. The name of the book is *Writing and Selling* by Mickey Spillane. The burden of his message was that the easiest thing to sell is a novel and the hardest, a short story. How do you write a novel? You take an existing, published novel that you like, you break it down scene by scene, and then you write your own characters and settings into this same format. If you can write, the method is foolproof. I tried it with a book that shall remain nameless (we all have our pride) and was met with immediate success after four years of messing around with rejection slips for my short stories. My agent, Ann Watkins, placed the novel with Doubleday.

After you sell a book pleasing things begin to happen. You are assigned an editor by the publisher, which means you can sit in the reception room without feeling like a supplicant on the road to Damascus. My editor was Stewart Alsop, whom I knew on the outside. We had a jolly time of it, arranging lunches for ourselves on Doubleday to select a suitable title. We hit on the title at the first lunch, but then had three or four more just to make sure we were right.

The title we chose was *Revelry by Night* from *Childe Harold's Pilgrimage*. The idea of the book was the similarity between the Brussels ball before the battle of Waterloo and the frivolous scene in the United States while Hitler played Napoleon in Europe. It was a big theme, which was the only thing that got me to write the book in the first place (you can't go to all that trouble just to write a who-struck-John), but not much of it survived in the published edition except by inference. Basically my idea was that Civilization, married to Democracy, gets fed up with the latter's flubbing around and succumbs to the lures of Nazi-Fascism, which in turn has no idea what to do with Civilization once the conquest has been made—a morality play in effect, born of my "World Perspectives" course. The protagonists for these various roles were a suburban housewife for Civilization, her stockbroker husband for Democracy, and an oddball sexist for the Nazi-Fascist type. Actually this little threesome got themselves in such convincing trouble that there was no need, from a story point of view, to spell out anything else. It was a natural for the hammock trade. The only thing that came through from the original concept was that the oddball sexist never screwed the girl on the beach when she was all laid out for his taking. This was meant to represent Nazi-Fascism not knowing what to do with Civilization after the conquest. I'm afraid all this got lost in the hammock and the poor fellow was just written off by the reader as some kind of backward pervert.

Nevertheless, the reviews were great. The first one I read was in *The New York Times.* It started off with the words "In a crisp, stinging, and sometimes savage first novel . . ." I put down the paper and drank in the sunshine. We were in Lenox having breakfast on the terrace of a house called Valley Head. The Berkshire Hills rolled off in front of us as far as the eye could see. That morning I felt the world was indeed my oyster.

Time magazine said "fluently readable and at times masterfully comic" and then went on to compare me with Hemingway, F. Scott Fitzgerald, and O'Hara. It seems incredible now, but at that point I had never heard of Fitzgerald. I remember saying to the agent, Ann Watkins, "I know about Hemingway and O'Hara but who is this guy Fitzgerald?" The reason, of course, was that after his early brilliance he had fallen out of the picture by 1940 and his revival was yet to come.

All this was grist to the ego and might well have gone to my head had it not been for a distressing little scene in Doubleday a week or so later. I had been asked in by one of the senior editors for a special congratulatory session in his office because the book was going so well. There I was sitting in a big leather chair nodding and beaming like a composite O'Hara, Fitzgerald and Hemingway when an underling approached the senior editor and whispered in his ear. I must say the editor was urbanity itself in the face of an embarrassing situation. It seems there had been a mistake. They had meant to call in the author of *Reveille in Washington*, which apparently was selling like hot cakes. He apologized, standing up too quickly I thought, considering the *bouleversement*—a kinder man might have offered a cigar—and what had been a most enjoyable situation suddenly went up in smoke. I mumbled my apologies, too, and slunk out the door.

That summer we chartered a ketch with some friends and cruised to Maine—Boothbay, Pulpit, Ragged Coat, and Northeast Harbors. On one of the early legs of the voyage we were headed for Boothbay after a night outside. The weather had cleared after a rather sticky, oily morning and the sunlight danced on the water. A strong breeze was off the quarter and a huge following swell made one think of the power of the sea, as it heaved up and receded behind us. We were headed for Seguin Light and could hear its great bullhorn long before we could see it. Then shortly we were up to it and swept past with the great swell running and the horn blasting and nothing else around. Passing Seguin Light was a memorable experience—the immensity of the sea bringing to mind the planetary nature of the world, and the bellowing insistence of the horn, my own (or anybody else's) ego.

I sold a second book to Doubleday the following spring. It was called *Land of Promise*. The title came from an article by Walter Lippmann in which he said that if America made a big effort and pulled itself up by its bootstraps, it could become the land of promise for mankind. I wrote him asking permission to use the quote, and he wrote back a one-liner saying he had no objection. This time, the girl (Civilization) was still married to her husband (Democracy), but she was fooling around with Communism in the form of a rather weedy Jewish intellectual. All this, of course, was somewhat of a rewrite of the first book. One hears that authors frequently go through life writing the same book over and over again. It is depressing, however, to recognize it in oneself.

As it turned out, no one else did. The book did as well as the first and the reviews were kind—I was an author to watch, etc.—but as soon as I gave it to Doubleday my interest died on the vine. With *Revelry by Night* I read the galley proofs with enormous pleasure in Central Park, savoring every minute under a tree on the grass. I never looked at the galleys of the second. Why? A drunk at a bar once told me you can get what you want in life, but when you've got it, there will be something wrong. There was— and it was World War II.

CHAPTER

Pearl Harbor found me at the Rockaway Hunt Club on Long Island, where their annual Gold Racquet Squash Tournament was in full swing. This weekend was always a festive affair with a large bibulous dinner at the club on Saturday night, followed by an equally bibulous brunch next day. The news on the radio Sunday morning had a definitely sobering effect.

I took a shower in the locker room that afternoon. There is something sybaritic about a good tiled shower bath, and these were the best, with large round heads on the showers through which the water poured down and literally drenched the person underneath. I took a long, hot soak, finishing off with an icy burst and thought "I will never see any of this again." There was something apocalyptic in the air.

Apocalypses were a little slower in those days. Nobody bombed New York, and after the initial shock, life seemed to go on much as usual. Bombing, however, was on everybody's mind. Sign painters must have made a fortune out of "Air Raid Shelter" signs which proliferated over the country. Usually, their authoritative arrows just pointed to a washroom, but the signs were comforting and made us look well-prepared.

Diana joined a group of wives in our apartment building

who went up to the roof each day to watch for aerial at-
tackers. People who should know have since told me that
no enemy plane of that time had the range to reach New
York. Still, we didn't know that, and it was all quite dramatic. I had a talk with Father about throwing in my
ROTC commission and joining the Marines as a private.
Father's reaction was abrupt. "Don't be a fool, boy," he
said. "You've got a commission. Keep it."

There was more than latent romanticism in this desire to
reject my commission. It was really only a polo commission, and I felt it would be bordering on the criminal to
subject the men under my command to my ineptitude with
artillery problems. These were no laughing matter. No
longer are the guns lined up on a ridge firing point-blank
into the oncoming infantry; that all went out with the Civil
War. In modern warfare you never see the enemy. Nowa-
days computers seek him out and destroy him, but at the
start of World War II it all depended on the ability of the
battery commander to master a series of complicated for-
mulas involving aiming points and observers. If the aiming
point was behind, you did one thing; if it was ahead, you
did another. Some people know this kind of thing instinctively. Not me. All I could think of was myself and battery
in an artillery duel with some little Jap and his battery invisible behind a hill. There would be the little Jap doing
lightning computations in his head, his shells falling with
deadly accuracy on our position, and there I would be lost
in a maze of foolscap as my men fell dead around me.

The problem was resolved, happily for me, by the mills
of the gods grinding exceedingly small. In the confusion following the outbreak of war, the War Department, as it was
then more straightforwardly called, went wild with its
mimeograph machine. One of the forms to be filled out list-
ed every disease known to man. As I had a rather pitiful
showing on this list, I felt I should put in something, so at

the end of a long row of allergies, none of which I had, under the heading "other" I carefully wrote in "champagne." Oddly enough, this particular handicap turned out to be anathema to the Army medicos who apparently had ruled that field artillerymen are not allowed to sneeze. I can't imagine what went on in their minds, unless it was the picture of some enemy agent plying me with Dom Perignon as the caissons went rolling along. In any case, the end result was that I was assigned to duty in Washington with Military Intelligence.

There was a man of parts in those days called Sir Robert Vansittart, a very dapper Englishman who was always seen at the races in gray topper and at all London balls, ballets and fetes in impeccable evening dress. A gadfly on the surface, he was nonetheless a big wheel in the Foreign Office— the prototype of "M" in the James Bond films. It seemed to Walter Mitty-like me that if I were going to be in Intelligence, here was a worthy model—a decorative spider sitting at the center of a vast net of sinister operations. It didn't quite work that way.

On reporting for duty in Washington, I spent the first night at the Hay-Adams Hotel and went out for a stroll in Lafayette Square before dinner, really to test my uniform and see if anyone saluted me. Everybody in uniform was saluting each other like crazy—all very enjoyable, like tipping your hat to a lot of new friends. When I returned to the hotel for dinner, the desk clerk handed me a message— "Please call at once." It was signed by a Colonel Rodriguez. My heart sank. I had put down on one of the innumerable War Department forms that I was fluent in French and Spanish, which was simply not the case, and here I was about to be found out by this wretched Rodriguez before I even reported for duty. I skipped the evening meal and spent the next two hours in an agonizing review of my Berlitz Spanish book, only to be told by the switchboard operator that it was all a mistake. The colonel wanted a Lieutenant Barnett.

The office to which I was assigned was in Counterintelligence. It kept track of enemy agents spying on us. There were four officers in the branch—the chief, and three others, each in charge of a so-called desk dealing with German, Italian, and Japanese espionage, representing our enemies of the day. A fourth desk was vacant and assigned to me. This was the Communist desk, which struck me as peculiar since Russia was presumably an ally and not an enemy at all. Here I was wrong. It is regrettable to say, but there was then, and there still is, an almost pathological fear of Communism in the United States. It is the big bugaboo that threatens to take away in one fell swoop everything we hold dear—God, the flag, motherhood, and all our shiny accessories. As no less a figure than Thomas Mann said twenty some years ago, "hysterical, irrational and blind hatred of Communism represents a danger to America far more terrible than native Communism."

The army mentality is peculiarly prone to worry about Communism. In Counterintelligence our chief source of information was the FBI. A stack of its material would appear on my desk each day—reports on the CIO, the Longshoremen, the Friends of the Abraham Lincoln Brigade, the League of Women Voters and so forth. In my day, the Bureau made little or no distinction between Communism and Socialism; both were un-American. So was any organization that smacked of liberalism, such as the American Civil Liberties Union and Americans for Democratic Action. The list of organizations alone made up a small booklet; Communists were believed to have infiltrated them all. Card files were kept on the interlocking directorships and the whole elaborately cross-indexed. I read reams of this material. If you overlooked the "alleged to be" caveats, you certainly got the impression that the country was about to be taken over by a massive Communist conspiracy. In the course of my duties I read the *Daily Worker* in the office, and occasionally would leave it in the men's room. Every time I did, the offending paper reappeared on my desk with a note attached from our security people: "Found in lavatory—Evidence of Communist infiltration." You have to admire the zeal.

In view of this background, the recent furor over CIA spying in the United States strikes me as ridiculous. High-powered committees are formed in the Executive branch and in Congress to search out the truth about this horrendous situation. Spying on Americans in the United States! Indignation runs high at this manifestation of police statism. How could this happen here? The plain fact is, as everyone knows, the FBI has been spying on Americans for years. Why pillory the CIA? The mechanism for a police state has always existed in the country ever since the FBI turned its hand to ideology. The only reason CIA activity was excluded from the United States, and many think illogically, was the prickly character of J. Edgar Hoover who would brook no outside meddling in his bailiwick.

The "irrational, blind hatred of Communism" cited by Thomas Mann was epitomized for me in a visit I paid to a doctor in Washington. I was suffering from hemorrhoids at the time and could neither sit, stand, nor lie down. As I was pacing about the doctor's reception room, I got into a conversation with his attractive blond nurse—a bit crisp, but obviously well-formed under her starched uniform. We talked about Russia and the Communist menace. The magazine in front of her was opened to an article which featured a map of the world with Russia at its center and around its periphery all the United States bombing bases with lines converging on Moscow. I pointed out that if the Russians had printed a similar map of the United States in one of their magazines, we would be horrified. All she did was glare at me fiercely. She was a real hysterical hater. The conversation had come to a standstill when it came my turn to see the doctor. After taking off my trousers and loosening my collar, we went into an inner sanctum with a prie-dieu arrangement in the middle, on which I was instructed to kneel. No sooner had I assumed a reverential position than the doctor pulled a giant lever and there I was with my tail in the air and my chin an inch from the floor. I have forgotten the order of insertion, but it seemed to me he had put in everything but the kitchen sink, light bulbs, and running water and was having a fine old time rummaging around when the telephone rang in his office. He stepped out, leaving me alone in my glory. I often view myself at the center of a comedy moving about me, but this was a bit much. At this juncture the crisp nurse stuck her head in the door. I maintained a dignified silence. There are certain positions from which you simply cannot argue.

After we moved into the Pentagon, the war for me became more intramural, both literally and figuratively. As everyone knows, the Pentagon is a five-sided building, but what the layman doesn't realize is that only the offices on the outside ring have windows. There are four other rings with offices in between and no windows at all, to which the workers and drones are relegated. Our branch drew one of these, which was all that could be expected in view of our humble rank in the hierarchy, but what made it impossible was that some civilian big shot out on the E ring with a window was gunning for us and trying to have us abolished because he needed the space for his people. One by one I watched my colleagues being shipped off to such patriotic and no doubt essential assignments as the quartermaster corps in Akron. When my turn came, it was to go to a place with the code name Dogpatch in Tennessee in some security capacity for the Manhattan Project. The latter might have been interesting in a negative sort of way—after all this was the atomic bomb—but I didn't like the idea of being pushed around. As a result I reacted in a most uncharacteristic fashion and took the bull by the horns, that is to say I marched into our persecutor's office on the E ring and told him that he needed me because of my unusual qualifications. Had he been a regular Army man, I would probably have ended up in a stockade. As he was not, he seemed to enjoy my approach.

"What, may I ask, are these unusual qualifications?"

I blurted out something to the effect that I knew a lot about Communism in the United States and that my education and background were such that I had a more balanced view on the subject than did the Army in general.

He sucked the end of his pencil for a moment, then nodded to his hatchet man who was standing beside me. "Jack," he said, "we'll keep him. Fix him up with a slot in the Russian group."

I went away delighted. The big shot was a man called Alfred McCormack who ran a hush-hush outfit in the Intelligence community known as the Special Branch. Everybody in it was very bright, and nobody ever said what they did. It was like joining an exclusive club. Actually the guts of the operation was out in the country where the enemy codes were broken by cryptographers in a large building surrounded by a double row of wire fences. Our job was to interpret their findings to the people running the war effort, starting with the President. Anything coming out of our office was automatically classified Top Secret—Ultra, which even in retrospect sounds impressive.

The rest of Army Intelligence detested this Special Branch and in particular Alfred McCormack, its chief. McCormack had been a partner in the Wall Street law firm of Cravath, De Gersdorff, etc. and was a personal friend of John McCloy, who in turn was a personal friend of FDR. Our line to the White House was solid. Army Intelligence tried to cut McCormack down to size by commissioning him a chicken colonel, but to no avail. McCormack continued to act as he had as a civilian—on the lieutenant general level at least. I don't go in much for leaders of men, but McCormack got through to me. He made me feel I was one of his boys.

As the war progressed, the Special Branch, like everything else, expanded. Amoebalike we subdivided into two units, one labelled "Political" and the other "Economic." Actually these were misnomers, as Political really meant Europe and Economic meant the Far East, and each unit covered the politics and economics of its area. Who we were fooling by this nomenclature I can't imagine. I suspect some chartmaker drew it up this way and it was too much trouble to change it. The Far Eastern unit contributed significantly to the war in the Pacific owing to the fact that the Japanese merchant fleet used a relatively simple code that was easy to break and so we could tell the Navy exactly where every ship was and where it was going. Towards the end of the war, the Navy was knocking off Japanese shipping at such a rate that many thought capitulation was imminent without the atomic bomb.

In the European unit I rose to be Deputy Chief of the Eastern European Section and held the rank of major. The Russians used something known as a "one time pad" for all their communications which was impossible to break because each time a new page of the pad was used as a key to the cryptography. As a result we had to confine our activities to the perusal of more open sources—newspapers, magazines, books, and so on. The only classified material of any value came from our embassy in Moscow. One evening at a dinner party in Georgetown, I overheard Diana chatting with Chip Bohlen. He had just been introduced as Ambassador Bohlen, and as I realized she had no idea of his stature in Russian affairs, I listened with some discomfort to her telling him that I was a Russian expert. It was painfully obvious that my expertise had not come to Bohlen's attention.

One rotating Branch assignment was to serve as night duty-officer in the Pentagon, which consisted of selecting items from the mass of incoming messages for presentation at the morning briefing. This took place at 7:00 A.M. and was quite an awesome affair. The Major General in charge, neat as a pin, sat behind an enormous desk flanked by two American flags and surrounded by what were known as the "twelve apostles"—a group of old-line army colonels who acted as an advisory council. The whole wall opposite them was taken up with a map of the world. The drill was that the duty officer would stand up smartly and read off his tidbits compiled during the night, and an enlisted man with a pointer would point to the appropriate place on the map where the event had occurred. It always seemed to me rather silly to point out Germany, France, Italy, and so on when we had items dealing with these countries, but that was the way the Major General liked it and that was the way it was done. I chose a splendid cable once that began: "Mullah Mustafa Barzani and the Kurdish chiefs are out to raid Shadad." The General was no great poet, certainly not a Kipling, but he had a sharp eye for detail. We had a nervous man with the pointer that morning and the end of it quivered on the map as he pointed out Iraq. The following day a mimeographed edict came down from on high which read "Henceforth, there will be no trembling with the pointer." I cite this merely to show what one can be up against in the Army.

As a reward for good behavior, officers in the Branch were sent abroad from time to time on assignment with the Joint Intelligence Collection Agency. In effect, the officers were merely armed guards for the pouches containing classified material. For this exalted role, we were issued a .38

revolver worn under the tunic in a shoulder holster. After conquering my initial fears that I might blow off my own hip, I then began to feel like an inept member of the Mafia. In order to get the gun out of the holster, I had to unbutton the top two buttons of my tunic and reach in under my tie, so by the time I could have gotten it in hand and aimed it, I certainly would have been dead.

A few days before V-E day, armed to the teeth in this fashion, I set off for France one night on a C-47 from Patuxent Naval Airbase. There were no other passengers on the plane and I found myself sitting on a lonely bucket seat in the dark. All the rest of the space in the cabin was taken up by giant crates of blood plasma, a very good thing when you need it, but something of a depressant when sitting with it in bulk. I tried to doze, but each time the pilot changed the speed of his motors I would sit bolt upright bracing myself for a sickening plunge in the sea. There was also something wrong with the port engine, like fire. Through a window partially obscured by one of the crates, I could see a flashlight being trained on the flaming exhaust. I watched it myself like a hawk long after the flame had subsided. Sleep was obviously out of the question, so feeling a need for human companionship I groped my way in the dark to the front of the plane. The navigator was startled when I opened the door between us and stumbled into his cramped quarters. "My God," he said, "where did you come from?" I must have cut quite a figure. Pale and shaky, I had taken off my tunic, but not the shoulder holster. The navigator recovered. "Check that gun," he said, "and I'll play you a game of gin." The rest of the crew were a studious lot and barely looked up from their comics as we hurtled through the night. I lost thirty dollars.

V-E day in Paris was wild, but not having slogged through the mud or heard a shot fired in anger, I felt like a ringer in the abandoned crowds on the Champs Elysées. I left them after an hour or so to solace myself with dinner at a restaurant off the Etoile. Although the price was fabulous, befitting the occasion, the meal itself was out of this world—Crème Gaulloise, rognons de veau in a superb sauce and the whole thing topped off by a coolly fresh mountain of fraises des bois sprinkled with powdered sugar. Over a brandy and a Monte Cristo No. 4, I surveyed my fellow diners. None of them looked in the least battered by the war, and I concluded that I had wound up in a nest of profiteers. One table in particular struck me because of its imbalance. A handsome young Frenchman in civilian clothes accompanied by three spectacular girls was ordering everything in the house. It made me shudder to think of his bill, but then I guessed it was worth it. They were obviously headed for an orgy. I watched them enviously for a while, then paid up and started the long walk back to my lonely hotel bed to the strains of the Marseillaise coming from the next block.

Rome was entirely different. In Paris, obviously, you could have had anything you wanted for a price. The French are so intrigued by La Belle Epoque that I think it will always survive, anyway in the food line. Not so in Rome. Shortly after my arrival I ran into a fellow on the street I used to know vaguely in school. His name was Pecci-Blunt and his sisters were giving a soirée that night in their Renaissance palazzo, to which he kindly invited me. The affair couldn't have been more sumptuous, in every detail but one. Footmen in powdered wigs lined the marble stairs holding lighted candelabra, violins played while fountains splashed in the gardens, and droves of noble Romans drifted through the festive scene. Champagne, whiskey and gin were everywhere in abundance. The only food to be had, however, came straight from the United States Army cafeteria. There was only one dish and it was tastefully served on giant silver salvers, but despite its elegant garniture SPAM is SPAM for all of that.

My hotel in Rome was the Medici-Hasler, a shoddily grandiose building at the top of the Piazza di Spagna. The massive square columns in the main lobby were nothing but beaverboard painted to look like marble, which may or may not be significant. The hotel was built in the heyday of the Nazi-Fascist pact.

The day following the Pecci-Blunt party I was walking down the steps to see a Colonel Smith who had an office overlooking the Trevi fountains. A girl walking ahead of me caught my eye because of her unusual appearance. Although tall with a willowy figure and the epitome of chic, her bare legs were covered with long, downy hair. I discovered later that hairy legs were a fad of the times, probably due to a shortage of razor blades. She stopped to look in a bookshop window on the ground floor of the building where I was going. A few minutes later, while sitting in the colonel's waiting room, I heard footsteps on the stairs and, looking through the open door, saw that she was coming to the same place. As she entered the waiting room I was called into the colonel's inner office, but as I went, we exchanged smiles and this time I took in her proudly handsome Italianate face, the dark eyes and aquiline nose.

The colonel turned out to be quite a jolly fellow, very sharp, too. I presented him with a letter signed by the major general who had taken such exception to any trembling with the pointer. It was an impressive letter explaining that I was on a special mission for the Military Intelligence Service, Washington, and that all possible assistance should be given me in the collection of political and economic information on the areas through which I was travelling. All hogwash really, but a nice thing to have in one's reticule.

Colonel Smith spotted it as hogwash. "What a lot of crap," he said. "Who would you like to see?" As I was not immediately forthcoming, he looked at me quizzically. "How about the Pope?" he suggested.

This seemed to me rather exalted fare, but I said it would be fine if he could manage it.

"I'd like to try," he said. "I'll see what I can do."

It seemed that over the past year Colonel Smith had been providing several influential Italians with such essentials as cigarettes and shoes from Army sources, and he wanted to test their presumed cooperation.

"How's Rome treating you?" he asked, leaning back in his chair.

"I've only just arrived," I said, "but I seem to have made a contact. As a matter of fact she's now in your outer office."

The Colonel rose and opened his door, then burst out laughing.

"My God, not that one. She used to work for the Germans. Maria!" he called. "How are you? I'll see you in a minute."

In the course of that minute I was quickly briefed on Maria. Her father had been a big-time clothes manufacturer in Milan; in fact, his factory had turned out most of the uniforms for the Italian Army. Her mother was a descendant of the last doge of Venice. As a young girl, she had been married to one of the top members of the Fascist hierarchy, but he contracted syphilis on the side and used to beat her. She got divorced and worked for the Italian Red Cross, a big thing in the early days of the war. She still loved everything German, but now was working for us.

The colonel opened the door again and was gallantry itself as Maria joined us for coffee. I gather she dropped in on him once or twice a week to pass the time of day and exchange a little gossip. She had a lot of dash and was obviously used to handling men. In no time at all I found I had asked her to lunch. The colonel had another engagement, so off we went together. Lunch was followed by tea at a sidewalk cafe, then later by dinner in one of Rome's cellar restaurants. Maria was quite a talker, completely fluent in English with only a trace of accent. I listened in fascination.

She had been assigned by the Italian Red Cross to work with Rommel's Afrika Korps, and there she met a young German interpreter named Willi with whom she had fallen in love. The two of them used to drive out in the desert in an old Isotta touring car and make love in the back seat, while tank warfare ranged around them. Maria's eyes flashed with reminiscence. "Ah the desert," she said, "that was a gentleman's war." The war, however, turned into a less gentlemanly affair as the Afrika Korps was pushed out of Africa. What had once been an elite outfit ended up in Italy reinforced by the dregs of the Wehrmacht. At this point she and Willi deserted, choosing for their hideaway a hill town with the symbolic name of Ama. Pursuit, of course, was inevitable. An Italian major, she said, rapped on their door one morning. Maria laughed happily. "I'm Italian and I know Italians. I told him that if he tried to take us I would shoot myself and Willi. 'Two lives, Signore Maggiore, and for what?' " The major was apparently a romantic because, according to Maria, tears welled up in his eyes. "Viva l'amore!" he said and, saluting smartly, marched out of the house.

The Germans were more difficult. Again it was a major, but this time with four storm troopers and there was no nonsense about the sanctity of love. Both she and Willi had their arms twisted behind their backs the moment they got inside. "I had to think quickly," said Maria. "When I was married we used to go to house parties with high-ranking Germans. There was one, a General Wolf, who later became head of Army Intelligence for Italy—crazy man, he once shot out all the street lamps on the main street of

Como. I had his army phone number and told the German major that we were working behind the lines for General Wolf. I gave him the number. If he doubted me, he could call up the General then and there. Well you know the Germans—he wasn't about to do that."

Maria confessed a lack of knowledge of how to deal with the British. Italy was out of the war, but Willi, as a German, was still fair game and was carted off to prison camp with a curt "Step lively, there." A week later he made his break. That night the English commander was displaying his camp to some visiting brass, and as the searchlights played over the empty compound, they came to rest on a neat, round hole. Willi by then was ensconced in the Vatican. His father had been the leader of the Catholic Centrist Party in Germany and, with the Nazi rise to power, had sent Willi to the Vatican to complete his schooling. As a student there, Willi returned out to be such a bad actor that the Vatican soon decided that he was not cut out for the cloth and packed him back to Germany. Arriving home, he had been immediately picked up and assigned to Rommel's staff as an interpreter. All-forgiving, the Vatican had granted him asylum. It was sort of an "old boys" return.

I met Willi a few days later. In the meantime, Colonel Smith's contacts had borne fruit, and I was handed one morning an impressive note with the keys of St. Peter embossed in the left-hand corner, inviting me to a private audience with the Holy Father who at that time was Pius XII. Having no idea where the Pope would be in the Vatican, I had the jeep drive up to St. Peter's, which was not the right place at all and made me a little late. The court chamberlain was waiting for me in the doorway of a nearby palazzo and looked at me severely from under his white-plumed hat. Maria, who had come along for the ride, blew me a kiss and settled back in the jeep to read her morning paper.

Inside the building the chamberlain and I squeezed into a tiny elevator and slowly ascended to the next floor. For some inbred reason I took off my hat in the elevator as if I were in Saks Fifth Avenue. Opening off the stair landing, where we came to a stop, was an enormous reception room, actually two big, square palace rooms bisected by a wide *allée*. On either side of this corridor ran a low, plush-covered railing. The room on the left was empty except for a massive chair enthroned on a raised dais; the room on the right was buzzing with GIs awaiting a public audience.

A pair of Swiss Guards stood at attention by the open doors at either end of the *allée* and, as the chamberlain and I entered, the four of them as one man brought their halberds to the salute. Dimly, out of the Officer's Manual, I remembered reading that you must have your hat on when saluting. I decided to disregard it and instead held my hat over my left breast in the approved civilian salute, and what's more, kept it there. Why, I will never know. We must have made quite a picture—the chamberlain in his white cockade walking a slow measured tread and me padding along behind him still holding my hat over my heart. By the time we got to the middle of the room, I heard one of the GIs mutter, "Who the hell is that jerk?" I began to wonder myself. Amongst other things, I had nothing to say to "Il Papa."

The chamberlain deposited me in the second room and with a stiff bow departed the way we had come. Lounging around on sofas and chairs were various members of the Noble Guard, that unit drawn from the noble families of Rome who traditionally serve the Pope in this capacity. Elegantly attired in white buckskin breeches, black leather hip boots and cuirasses, most of them seemed a little the worse for wear from a party the night before. Since I had been at the same party, I joined a small group that I recognized, which was gathered around an open window.

Almost immediately a new cicerone appeared, a short

pansy prelate in a red skullcap, under whose guidance I passed through a third salon, this time filled with red-capped cardinals and monsignori, some of them on their knees. Beyond the princes of the church was the private audience chamber, where my guide left me to myself. The room was considerably smaller than the others with a co-zier throne at one end and a row of flimsy gilt chairs against the walls. There was no rug on the parquet floor and the general effect, except for the throne, was that of a dancing class I used to attend in New York. I sat down on one of the gilt chairs.

After a short wait, a door opened in the wall to the left of the throne and an Italian family, the man in funereal black and the lady and her two daughters in white, backed out on the parquet followed by the Pope, a slender figure also in white, blessing their genuflections. They left by way of the room with the cardinals, and out of the corner of my eye I saw my cicerone who had reappeared in the doorway and was motioning me to drop to my knees. I did, and kissed the proffered pontifical ring, wondering at the same time if they dipped it in Dobell's solution. As it didn't seem to me we could have much of a conversation with me on my knees, I stood up, much to the consternation of my guide in the doorway.

"My son," said the Pope, "You are not Catholic." I re-plied in the negative, which I guess was unnecessary, and the Pope went on. His English, though halting, was infi-nitely better than my Italian. Colonel Smith must have enclosed the hogwash letter signed by the major general because the Pope immediately launched into an analysis of the political scene, the stress of which was that Commu-nism in Italy was winning its battle against the Church. "We need money," he said, and added almost conspira-torially, "we have organizations in your country. Would you bring this to their attention?"

I said I would and the Pope clapped his hands signaling

to the pansy prelate. "I would like to give you this medal," he said. I had an immediate vision of myself in white tie with a splendid Maltese Cross in enamel and gold on a watered silk red ribbon. Instead, I was presented with a miniscule medal about the size of a nickel, which in fact was not a medal at all, but some sort of commemorative coin. I bowed, and the Pope began walking to the door leading into the cardinal's room. Here ensued an embarrassing scene. Under the impression that he was going out to his public audience, I thought it only polite to let the Pope go first, but apparently he had some other method of getting there. After a brief mating dance like two ruffled grouse, I got the picture and managed to back out past him.

In the waiting jeep outside, Maria seemed impatient and had already told the driver to start the motor.

"What was it like?" she asked.

"He was interesting," I said. "Part ward politician and part ascetic saint." The latter was certainly true. The Pope's eyes were otherworldly, deep in their sockets, and he looked as though he had suffered.

"He has terrible hiccups," said Maria. "Let's go see Willi now."

In contrast to the great salons I had just left, Willi's refuge in the Vatican was a cell—a monastic cell to be sure, but still prisonlike in its austerity. High in one of the whitewashed walls was a low arched window with bars that admitted a pale gray light. There was a peg on the back of the door with Willi's cassock and a large black hat. The only other thing in the room was a cot with Willi on it, in his underwear, reading *Esquire* by the light of a naked bulb. He was short and blond and very muscular, but his eyes were what struck me at once, laughing and very mischievous. No chip off the old block, Willi was a wild one. After kissing Maria and greeting me, he immediately reached in under the cot and pulled out an enormous flagon.

"Vino?" he said. "Very good bladder medicine." He had a slight English accent.

We had to drink it out of the flagon with one finger hooked through the handle and its weight resting on the arm like a jug of cider. "Ein bruderschaft," said Willi. And it was. We had a few more, then dressed him up in his clerical disguise and went out to have some pasta before going to a concert in a nearby church. Pablo Casals was playing. In the middle of the concerto for violin and cello, I noticed Willi whispering to Maria. She clued me in. Apparently the English commandant of the camp from which Willi had escaped was sitting in the gallery and had spotted Willi in the orchestra.

They moved fast at intermission, slipping out a side door. The last I saw of those star-crossed lovers was in the alley outside the church. Maria was dragging Willi who had put on his big black hat and was pulling it down over his eyes, but not before giving me a wink. Looking most suspicious, the two of them vanished into the night. I flew out the next day.

Like many members of the armed forces during World War II, I was a noncombattant. I never saw a "buddy" killed. Possibly if I had, I would have felt more passionately about the war, but I doubt it. On the homeward flight which took off from London in the evening, I was again an isolated passenger and joined the pilot and crew in the cockpit. Up there the stars seemed more real than the void of ocean below. I jotted down the following:

> *When I look at Orion flanked*
> *By Sirius and Aldebaran,*
> *What possible cause on earth*
> *Could make me partisan?*

The pilot, a cherubic youth of twenty-two, read it over my shoulder.

"Say, Major," he said, "I think you've got something there."

CHAPTER

The day I stopped being an up-and-coming man dawned like any other. Following the war, I had moved over to the State Department with an elite group headed by Alfred McCormack, my old boss in the Special Branch. McCormack had ridden high in the Pentagon owing to the McCloy-FDR axis and confidently expected to do the same in State. He didn't. Nevertheless, my move under his aegis was the nearest I ever came to featuring in the pages of history. At that, it was not by name, but the fact was recorded on page 161 of Dean Acheson's *Present at the Creation*:

> On March 14, 1946 Rep. Andrew Jackson May [Chairman of the House Committee on Military Affairs] charged that persons with "strong Soviet leanings" who had been forced out of the War Department were now to be found in State . . . Col. McCormack [Special Assistant for Research and Intelligence] demanded retraction defending the persons—some twenty in all—brought over from Military Intelligence. The Appropriations Committee cut out his entire appropriation and on April 22, Col. McCormack submitted his resignation.

The moral of this is that if you hitch your wagon to a

Costumed as a major

star, be sure he doesn't get sacked. Actually, the charge was ludicrous; it was retracted and most of the appropriation was restored. The incident, however, is a perfect example of bureaucratic infighting. During the war, McCormack had trodden on a lot of toes, including those of the previously mentioned "twelve apostles" in Military Intelligence. He was also beginning to tread on some old-line State Department toes. The combination was lethal. All that had to be done was for someone to drop an innuendo to a man like May, who saw Communists under his bed, and the rest was automatic. Again the bugaboo. And this was long before Senator McCarthy.

In such a situation it's best to be inconspicuous. I couldn't have been more so. My office at the time was an outsized broom closet in the bowels of the old State Department building on Pennsylvania Avenue. I once passed General Marshall in the hallway upstairs, but that was the extent of my mingling with the Secretary of State. With McCormack's departure our group fell apart at the seams. Despite their alleged pro-Soviet leanings, most of the twenty returned to lucrative New York jobs in corporate law and finance.

Surveying my own survival kit, I decided it looked decidedly ill-equipped. At this point I probably should have charted a course in the government that would have enabled me to put into effect all the fine precepts they attempted to instill in us at school. But man is a weak reed in his approach. Besides, it seemed to me those precepts were primarily guidelines for people at some pinnacle of power. Looking at my own position, I saw this was not exactly the case. I had a medium-level job, which is all very well if you feel you belong to an elite group, but without such a group the job is just plain medium, and in my case it was even evanescent. Who on earth would hire me? My qualifications were not outstanding and I had an unfortunate quality of being able to view my superiors objectively, which is no good at all in any organization. Predating the young who were not yet born, I also had a sneaking suspicion that maybe the game was not worth the candle. Nevertheless, I was not about to take to the woods; I needed a job as a matter of straight survival. There were a lot of people like me, trapped by their own limitations. Fortunately, limitations are not emblazoned on our foreheads. I wangled a job in the Department's Office of Intelligence Research.

Mother died that year in New York. She had become more and more of a recluse. "Tired of livin', and feared of dyin' " summed up her approach to life. Never one with many friends, those whom she had were suffering through the remainder of their lives. Both her cousins had broken their hips. She used to visit them trying to cheer them up with lugubrious bits of gossip, thin work at best as most of their friends were dead, but then she could no longer do it and they couldn't come to her. She died on Christmas Day after a long siege with dropsy—alone, bored, and frightened. I had called her earlier from Washington with all the children lined up for cheery Christmas greetings, but the nurse told me she was asleep. Father called in the afternoon and I took the next train. He was sitting in the dining room reading the paper when I arrived. "De mortuis nil nisi bonum," he said, which struck me as odd even though I knew they had not gotten on for years. I went upstairs two flights to her bedroom. There was an open book face down on the bed. It was *A Christmas Carol*, which she used to read to me every Christmas Eve. Poor forgotten woman, clinging to a moment in the past during her final hours of waiting . . . I remembered her laughter at dinner parties, I used to sit on the stairs listening, but that was a long time ago . . . I thought of the plate I had thrown at her, of Father's disaffection. Then, as I stood there, what struck me was the total absence of person. There was a body, but nothing more. No dweller within, just a blank. I shut the door and went down to the library. The true WASP always keeps a stiff upper lip, but I was alone in the library staring at the gap in the set of Dickens where *A Christmas Carol* had been, and the lower lip took over. I blubbered. It was a long-forgotten sensation.

Following Mother's death, I inherited a little money. I still had to work, but I could take a taxi without thinking about it, a lesser version of Mr. Morgan's quip about owning a yacht. Nonetheless, something slipped a notch when most of my elite group in the Department went on to better things. To use an old-fashioned expression, I began to feel I was not going to make my "Y" in life, yet my inner friend (my soul?), was not bothered by such considerations.

The job in the Research Office was really an exercise in psychology. I was editor of their Current Intelligence Digest, one of those unwanted daily brochures that clutter up the in-baskets of busy men. Although it went to a lot of impressive people, it seemed to me most unlikely that anyone ever read it. No man with a knotty problem is going to dwell for long on the fact that the fruit pickers in Afghanistan are growing restive. We had a lot of little gems like this. The sweat and tears that went into the construction of these items was unbelievable. The authors were usually PhDs or else had completed all the requirements for the degree except the final thesis. All of them, even the weediest, were consumed with intellectual arrogance, and, in my opinion, the most ill-founded arrogance. In the first place I had usually never heard of the institution where they had gotten or were getting their PhDs. This I suppose was a trifle arrogant on my part but you've got to fight fire with fire. Secondly, learned men though they were in their own particular disciplines, they were almost totally inarticulate when it came to putting their thoughts on paper. Incidentally, I hate this use of the word "discipline." To me it should be used only in its crisp, martial sense as in "no discipline all up and down the line," but the Groves of Academe have taken over the word and would be lost without it. I suppose they're entitled to this more unctuous usage, but it was another bone of contention between us.

Our editorial sessions were similar to bullfights. The door would open and in would come the arrogant PhD, not physically snorting and pawing the carpet with his feet, but psychologically these were his emanations. I would be sitting with his brainchild in front of me and figuratively we would have a few passes with the cape. "A fine piece," I would say just to get him to sit down. Not having a PhD myself, or any of the requirements, I didn't want to be gored in the first skirmish. Once seated, I would let him have a touch of the banderillo. "That first paragraph," I would say, "seems to me unnecessary." The academician would usually roll his eyes as if pleading with some unseen deity to deliver him from the hands of the infidel. "What are we trying to put across?" I would continue. "Basically, the fruit pickers are growing restive. Right?" Grudgingly, this would be admitted. "Then we don't really need that bit about court practices under Tamurlane." Again the eyes to heaven, but my sword was poised for the kill. "It has to go," I would say, and leaning well over the manuscript, I would plunge my pencil in his heart. Sometimes I muttered "Olé!"

There was another "bullfighting" editor in an adjacent office named Roger Dow. We were just two against a big herd in our building, and we became inseparable. When Zeno was asked what a friend was, he replied "Another I" and that was Roger. We saw alike on everything. He was a trifle sedentary in his habits, which combined with a passionate love of food, drink and tobacco brought him to an untimely end, but we had several glorious years. We ate lunch together daily. Over our first one, he struck me as a man of truth. Before the war he had been an assistant instructor at Harvard—i.e., on the lowest rung of the academic ladder where a PhD was the highest. Now he dominated them in the ring. "It has taken a world conflagration," he said, "to obliterate my humble past. I am grateful." He was a clear thinker and articulate, two rare qualities in our particular branch of the national effort.

By the time the Joe McCarthy hearings came along, we had developed a flawless lunch technique. We would convene on the second floor of the Metropolitan Club. Under the solicitous eye of Bob, the bartender, we would consume two and sometimes three martinis on the rocks while rolling for the check. We played a complicated game of our own involving ten dice. It must have been invented by the English in some place like Kuala Lumpur, as it took forever to finish. From time to time we joined another table in the bar where Arthur Krock used to relax after interviewing the great. There they played the more usual five dice game. If you rolled five aces in one roll (the chances against which are astronomical) you had to buy a drink for everyone at the table. You were rewarded, however, by having your name inscribed on a silver plaque which hung on the wall above the table. I achieved this once years later when I was no longer living in Washington, but had just dropped in for the day. It was a form of immortality that poor Roger never made. He had few aspirations in life, but this was one of them. And at that time the rolls seemed limitless.

Following the cocktail period—the Dean Achesons and the Averell Harrimans had long since had their drink, eaten lunch, and were reshaping the world—we would repair to the downstairs dining room to order oysters, hamburger and a beer. Entertainment was provided by a TV set high in the wall with McCarthy scowling and droning his accusations, but the hamburgers were really the *pièces de résistance.* We would place on top of each a raw onion ring from which the center had been removed and into this empty space pour ketchup, A-1 and a drop of Tabasco. After sprinkling lightly with salt and pepper, we would gaze appreciatively at the neat concoction held in place by the onion ring and then squash it down with the buttered top of the English muffin. It took a lot of paper napkins to get through one hamburger, but they were ambrosia. Like so much in life, however, two of them were too many.

In the course of living in Washington, Diana and I had five different houses in Georgetown, and of the five, I owned three at one time, which was a little hair-raising until we sold the other two. You could live in a Georgetown house for a while, then sell it, not for an enormous profit, but enough so that you could say you lived in it free for a year or two. Our first house was on Dumbarton Avenue across the street from Joe Alsop. The street was a little more ramshackle then. On one of our early exploratory walks, I remember a dilapidated wooden house with a front porch on which an elderly colored couple were sitting in rocking chairs. As we passed by eyeing it speculatively, the old man observed to his companion, "Lawdy, Lawdy . . . More white folks pushing out blacks."

Georgetown then had not quite reached its boom state. Old brick houses of the Federal period were still available with panelling downstairs and a potential garden in the rear. Ours was not quite up to this category, being very small, but then chic is determined more by what you put into the box than by the shape of the box itself. We had the Sheraton sideboard, and we only lacked a decent dining room table, ten Duncan Phyfe chairs, and a crystal chandelier to make it the perfect setting for a small, diplomatic dinner. You can do a lot with candles, but our first attempt at a chic little dinner lacked a certain polish. This defect was due to the cramped quarters and flimsy construction rather than the lack of furniture. As sometimes happens at the best of parties, there was a sudden lull in the conversation into which void came the unmistakable sound upstairs of the nurse's rump grinding into the bathtub. It's a difficult thing to gloss over.

So much nesting produced two more daughters in two years. I am not against children per se, we always wanted a family at some point, but contraceptive failure of such proportions was a crippling blow to the economy. Diana got a job in a bookstore, which barely paid the wages of the nurse. We had to move to another house, and instead of Duncan Phyfe, there was now an overflow of cribs and potty chairs and all the horrid objects needed for the raising of the young. Some people, strong, good men, love to nuzzle little babies, crooning with pleasure at the bodily contact. I find little babies repulsive. I like children well enough when they begin to talk as individuals, but not before. I used to take long walks with the dogs who didn't warm to babies either.

Sometimes, however, I would gather my brood together before an open fire and read to them from the telephone book. The fact that they enjoyed these readings proves a point. Their eager little upturned faces were really quite endearing as I intoned through a batch of Mushinskys—Albert, David, Frederick, Morris (2), and Peter—then Hillel Mushowitz and the Mushroom Corporation of America. They appeared genuinely distressed when I closed the good book.

About this period in our lives, Diana with some justification accused me of total disregard for the well-being of our progeny. She had gone shopping in New York for a few days and, although I had been left in charge, I must admit the children were not uppermost in my mind. This was because her departure seemed to me an ideal opportunity to do a little remodelling of our living room that I had been secretively plotting for some time. The room was a difficult one: the staircase came straight down into it, ending up about two feet from the fireplace. This situation I felt could be improved by turning the stair at right angles about four steps up and putting in a wall between it and the fireplace. From time to time, to achieve what one wants, one has to act independently in a household. Diana, I knew, would have vetoed the project, but she would enjoy the finished product. It would be a nice surprise for her when she got back.

Everything had been worked out in advance with the precision of a D-day plan. As I left Diana at Union Station (the air shuttle had not yet been thought of), workmen at that very moment were scheduled to move into the house.

It's an odd thing about remodelling—reconstruction takes forever, but demolition takes no time at all. By the time I got back from the office that evening the staircase in its entirety had been ripped out and in its place was a rough painter's ladder stretching up to the second floor landing. It seems that the struts, or whatever the wooden supports of a staircase are called, were rotten and needed replacement. The foreman had called me and I, never thinking of the children getting over their colds on the third floor, had told him to do the necessary. As I came in, peering down the hole from above was the aged crone we had hired as a nurse and the two youngest children whose legs, I knew, would never reach the rungs of the ladder. In short, they were all trapped—and starving. To make matters worse, Diana called me that evening to say she was coming back two days earlier than intended. Needless to say, by the time she returned the ladder was still *in situ*. The nurse, who had been gotten up and down with some difficulty, had departed as soon as Diana returned.

If one doesn't have a predilection for the role of pater familias and no consuming interest in an outside career, where is one at? Mr. Thoreau may have put his finger on it with that bit about most men living lives of quiet desperation. I don't think all is lost; there is no real reason to be desperate, you just have to make an adjustment to the fact that most of life is led in the interstices of accomplishment. If you look at a big net, there is more empty space than string, and that's where most of us live. I'm not addressing myself to those who thrive on competition or have a clear-cut goal towards which they are headed. They may be too busy tightening the skeins of the net to enjoy the space in between.

One night I was deep in an interstice. I had risen about 4:00 A.M. and was sitting on the john gazing into the bathtub at the hopeless struggle of a cockroach attempting to climb out of the tub. He would do very well about three-quarters of the way up the side and then fall back to the bottom. Each time he fell back he would shake himself, gather his forces together, and try the ascent again. I admired his pluck and grit, but I didn't really want him out of the tub and running all over the house. And yet, like the Jains in India who wear gauze masks over their mouths to avoid killing an insect while breathing, I felt it would be wrong to squash him. (As the old song goes, a duck might be somebody's mother.) It was late but I called a friend, J. B. White, who kept all sorts of hours and I knew would enjoy the problem. Following considerable philosophic discussion—presumably the insect prefers whatever it is doing to extinction—we decided that it was entirely unsuitable for man to assume the role of God and capriciously take a life. The cockroach must be spared. The solution was to run the water in the tub and flush him down the drain. It couldn't be too bad; after all that's where he came from. He probably ran away from his wife and children. We would make him a better cockroach. Both of us felt quite strongly that the Jain priests in Calcutta should reserve two niches for us in their pantheon of saints.

An opportunity arose about this time to improve my situation in the Department. I applied for and got an assignment with the splendid title of "Intelligence Advisor to the Bureau of European Affairs." The job had been created by the Wriston Committee, a Presidential study group formed to tighten up the workings of the Executive branch. In its wisdom, the Committee had decided that one of the imperfections of State could be rectified if the Intelligence people were brought into closer contact with the operating people. The job was an improvement on my editorial "bullfighting" days, but not much. We never had any "intelligence" to offer that the operating people didn't already know. I would attend the daily staff meeting of my Assistant Secretary of State in which the various Branch Chiefs would brief him on what was happening in their areas. After going around the table, the Assistant Secretary would turn to me wearily and ask the *pro forma* question, "Does Intelligence have any light to throw on the subject?" to which I would have to say "No." The trouble was that the operating people received the same intelligence reports that I did. I often thought that if I could remove their names from the distribution list, I might occasionally come up with something. The chances even then were remote. The amount of intelligence material that daily ended up in the "circular file," as the classified wastebasket was called, was absolutely staggering. The staff meetings had no time for it. They were kind to me, however, and let me share their coffee.

Meanwhile life in Georgetown continued to be delightful, all very small town and convivial. There were a few stars amongst our acquaintance, all assistants to Dean Acheson, but mostly it was made up of small-fry WASPs like ourselves who had stayed on after the war. Some were "cliff dwellers" (i.e., those who had always lived in Washington), but the majority had come from other urban centers. We were bound together by the ties of shared schools, colleges, clubs, mutual friends and relations—in essence, a permanent strata within a society traditionally in flux.

Morgan's drugstore at the corner of 28th and "P" Street had a bulletin board with handwritten notes announcing the birth of hamsters, changes of address, and the need for baby sitters. In winter we played squash, skated on the old C&O canal, and danced at the Sulgrave Club; in the spring and fall there were waltz parties, picnics, tennis, touch football, and dog walking in Rock Creek Park. We had one long walk called the Witch's Walk that used to intrigue the children. It started in Montrose Park, continued down through massive oaks that brought to mind Sherwood Forest and Robin Hood, descended to Rock Creek and up again through what was then woods and fields behind Wisconsin Avenue. In one of the fields, there was an old dead tree that looked like an Arthur Rackham drawing. It had weird tentaclelike branches and a dark cavernous hole in the center. The two younger children were never quite certain whether a witch lived in it or not. Rock Creek Park in those days was a far less sinister place than it has become lately. One of our friends was raped while walking her dogs, but that was at a much later date. For the most part, incidents in the Park areas were confined to an occasional murder or suicide with no racial overtones. We had our quota of queers and transvestites lurking about in the bushes, but the times were gentler then. I may be guilty of representing the "good old days" as a "Golden Age," but consider the urbanity and polish of the following little scene.

The children of friends of ours, two brothers aged ten and seven respectively, were approached one afternoon by a middle-aged gentleman exposing himself. The man made himself quite clear to the older brother asking him to join him in a tryst down the road. The older boy replied politely, but firmly, saying, "Thank you very much, but I don't care to." At this point the exhibitionist looked crestfallen. "How about your brother?" he asked hopefully. The older boy shook his head again. "No thank you," he said, "I don't think he would care to either." The middle-aged man understood class when he saw it and walked off disconsolately, zipping up his fly. When the boys were asked later for a description of the man, all that came out was that he was a gray sort of gentleman who looked as though he had gone to Harvard. Obviously, these were a dime a dozen.

The British Foreign Office used to classify the District of Columbia as a tropical post. To combat the extreme heat, I built a swimming pool one summer in the back yard of our house at 3235 "R" Street. It was not a real swimming pool —the industry was still in its infancy—it was more a glorified outdoor bathtub, but it served the purpose. We were building up a terrace at the back of the house and, rather than filling in all of it, I left an oblong hole which was lined with cement. Its length was as long as I am with my arms outstretched; the width was determined by my sitting on the bottom and stretching out my legs to touch the other side; the depth, also based on this position, was as much water as it took to come up to my chin. Filled by a hose, it could be emptied by pulling an old-fashioned rubber plug thereby watering the lawn. The whole thing looked quite decorative with the palest of blue interior paint and pink azaleas along one side. I used to sit in it nude at night with a drink and a five-pound chunk of ice floating in the water beside me. Some of my happiest moments in the nation's capitol were spent in this position, contemplating the play of light on a giant Dumbarton oak that had somehow strayed in years gone by and ended up in our garden.

During my State Department career I began to feel like General Braddock who had all those horses shot out from under him at the battle of Montreal. I had moved to another job in the Bureau of European Affairs, and my experience with it illustrates a basic bureaucratic law. This time I had another good title—Officer in Charge of European Defense Community (EDC) Affairs. The EDC, when I got it, was still very much in its formative stages, being nothing much more than a concept. But then it began to develop, and as it took on flesh and blood, you might think my fortunes would soar. Quite the reverse. The law is this. The moment a subject becomes important, higher and higher bureaucrats zero in on it with the inevitable result that the fellow who had it in the first place becomes entirely superfluous. This happened to a friend of mine who had the Korean "desk" when nobody ever thought of Korea. His problem was greater than mine, however, as everybody from President Truman and General McArthur on down got into the act before that one was finished. I only had the Secretary of State, the Assistant Secretary for Europe, my Chief of Branch, the Assistant Chief of Branch, my Section Chief and assorted Pentagon types and economists—all of whom became authorities on the EDC overnight. As low man on the totem pole I had virtually nothing to do.

When working for the government in a humble job, one can sometimes achieve a certain status by letting slip, inadvertently of course, the idea that the humble job is just a cover for one's highly secretive and important activities. From time to time you read in the paper of some humdrum little man who for years has been running a shoe store in Kent, but on his deathbed he turns out to be a former member of the German General Staff and chief of the Abwehr for Britain. That kind of thing has always intrigued me. *Faute de mieux*, I made it my own approach, but aside from a few impressionable dinner partners, I don't think anyone was fooled.

Diana, on the other hand, was doing extremely well in another field of endeavor. That winter *Life* came out with a central spread in color of seven young Washington hostesses of which she was one, looking very pretty and chic. In the blurb under the photograph she was described as wearing a short organza evening gown (Ben Reig) and as the wife of a State Department specialist. Obviously the blurb writer considered what she was wearing as more important than to whom she was married. As a male chauvinist, I suppose I would have preferred to see "wife of the new dynamic director of ———, wearing her olive drab." Not that I was jealous, we worked as a team—I held up my end with the ladies, and since I was a good listener, I could always talk to anyone—but the fact that our social life was so much bigger league than my role within the government gave me a momentary pang. I decided not to fret it. We once gave a party in honor of Brian de Bois Gilbert. (He was the Knight Templar in *Ivanhoe*.) It was surprising how many people knew the family, but not Brian himself. We hired a suit of armour for the hall, just to refresh their memories.

In all organizations some people are masters at making bricks without straw, but I have never been good at it. Since my talents were buried under a top-heavy bushel, I occupied my time in the office writing a cookbook, or more precisely, a dictionary of culinary terms. It was filled with useful information for those who want to know what they're getting in for when faced with a fancy French menu—such things as "argenteuil" means asparagus; "clamart" means peas; "florentine," spinach; "parmentier," potatoes; and so on. It would have made a marvelous stocking present, being long and narrow to fit into inner pockets, but as it needed amusing sketches and this was not my forte, I considered other lines of endeavor. I should be more patriotic; one practically owed it to the country to make a killing in something. I thought of forming the American Bidet Company; the bathroom was the citadel of the American home and everybody who was anybody should have one. It was just a matter of overcoming the prejudice that somehow a bidet was a dirty French object. Another scheme was to build a small club on Cabo San Juan, Puerto Rico. I had just finished reading a report called "Operation Bootstrap" and felt that Puerto Rico and I were in the same boat. The property I wanted was on the northeast tip of the island and, when they finished their new jet airport and super-highway, it would be readily accessible to winter visitors. I had in mind $25,000 for the land. It was something of a shock, therefore, when the owner turned out to be a real Spanish *hidalgo*, living off pre-Armada money, who wouldn't consider anything less than $250,000! Recounting the venture to my father when I went up to see him in New York, I thought he would be proud of his son's attempt to break out of the mold and do something active. Instead, he went ashen, which was worrisome as he had been ailing, and it wasn't until he heard the outcome that he heaved a sigh of relief. "Stick to your last, boy," he said. "You're no business man." He was right, of course. Nevertheless, occasionally I take out the prospectus and gaze at it fondly. In one section describing the facilities, I wrote that the club bar would be open until closing. It could have been a splendid place.

Returning to my last, which needless to say I had never left during all this thrashing about, I decided to do some serious, independent writing in the greater WASP tradition. That there was something definitely wrong with overall United States policy seemed to me undeniable. The more I thought of it, the more I felt (as writers do sometimes) that I was uniquely qualified to write about it. The year was 1953 and the country was in the grip of purposeless forces whose only major goal was to "contain" Communism. Furthermore, if that was our goal, it seemed to me we were going at it in the wrong way.

Our foreign policy should be to keep Russia and mainland China apart insofar as possible. Bolstering up Chiang Kai-shek on Formosa would have the opposite effect of bringing them closer together. And that was what we were doing. Instead, I felt we should forget about Chiang and concentrate our efforts on exacerbating relations between Russia and China itself. Although I didn't know what they were, I was certain there must be many bones of contention between them and that it wouldn't be too hard to get the two countries snarling at each other.

After conducting some private research, I turned up quite a few potential trouble spots and areas of fundamental disagreement. Undoubtedly there were many more that the experts could develop, but I assembled enough to make my point clear.

The long border between the two countries was an absolute natural for trouble. Ranging from the Amur River in the east, where zealous border guards lined both sides, to Sinkiang Province in the west, where half a million Kazakh tribesmen could be a disruptive factor owing to the adjacent Kazakh S.S.R., there were numerous tender places. When the Russians pulled out of Manchuria in 1946, for example, they removed large quantities of machinery. They offered replacements, to be sure, but the Chinese Communists had to pay for them. The Chinese felt that Manchuria and everything in it was theirs after the Japanese defeat. So did the Russians. Moving west, there was the problem of the two Mongolias: Russia wanted to take over Inner Mongolia (it's "inner" to China) and the Chinese were eyeing Outer Mongolia where the Russians had been dominant since the seventeenth century. We didn't have much to go on—we had only one unverified intelligence report of the massacre of a Chinese border garrison while asleep—but one thing was certainly true, relations between the two Communist giants were far from sweetness and light despite the official pronouncements of Sino-Soviet friendship. All the ingredients were there to produce a flare-up; they only needed a catalyst. Within the Communist movement, there was the pre-eminence of Mao as theoretician opposed to the upstart Khruschev. The Chinese Communists with their strong national pride disliked the patronizing attitude and technical superiority of the Russians, whom they regarded as immature barbarians. They still remembered their 1927 experience with Russia when they supported Chiang on orders from Moscow, only to be hunted down by Chiang later. When finished, I felt that I had put together a logical presentation, the obvious conclusions of which were a complete reversal of our support for Chiang Kai-shek.

President Eisenhower's Special Assistant for National Security Affairs, Robert Cutler, was the uncle of a girl, Mary Cutler, who used to work on the same staff that I did back in my "bullfighting" days. Through her, I got my paper to Uncle Bobby. You couldn't go any higher. About a week later I got back my opus with a note attached saying, "Read with interest. Thanks very much (signed) Robert Cutler." I comforted myself with Emerson's thought—"no member of a crew was ever praised for the rugged individualism of his rowing." The following day all the papers carried banner headlines proclaiming CHIANG UNLEASHED! I felt something of a misfit.

I didn't know quite what my expectations were. I never really thought that the National Security Council would rise as one man and say, "By George! This fellow's got something!" and recall the Seventh Fleet. I was a maverick so far down the chain of command that I was nearly out of it. China was really none of my business, I had no standing, I was not even in the Bureau of Far Eastern Affairs. Why did I write it? I suppose out of a sense of perversity. Everybody was talking about the new Soviet-Chinese monolith. Most of them were the same kind of people who were terrified of Communism at home. They simply couldn't be right.

Nor were they, as events have proved. The Soviet-Chinese monolith was still a bugaboo a decade later when we began to pour money, men and supplies into Indo-China in order to stop the monolith from sweeping through Southeast Asia. The monolith literally had to blow up in our face before we could see that the *casus belli* was a myth. At the risk of sounding smug, the blowup came as no surprise to me. The strange thing is that over the years there must have been people in the government who also knew that the monolith concept was a fraud. Where were they? The old "China Hands" had been purged, but there must have been others. Maybe not. Maybe nobody thought about it at all—a frightening thought in itself considering the lives and treasure wasted fighting a nonexistent menace. A kinder theory would be that the arteries of government had become so hardened that no ideas contrary to official thinking could circulate upwards. If you take a Puritan base, add a touch of Senator McCarthy, a pinch of xenophobia, and stir in well with the military-industrial complex, you have official thinking. Could it be that we, like the Russians, are barbarically immature? The answer, of course, is yes. Sophistication has never been high on our national list of priorities. I used to brood about the inevitability of a nuclear holocaust. The dweller within my body couldn't have cared less.

CHAPTER

Shortly after this abortive flight in the stratosphere of policy, I joined the Foreign Service.

It is a fact of life that if you don't have an urge to push others around, you will be pushed around yourself. During my post-formative years in Washington it seemed to me that I was always moving from pillar to post because of this flaw in my character. Life outside of the so-called working hours was delightful but, like Mr. Micawber, my career was in need of a deus ex machina. It came in the form of a sweeping reorganization of the State Department proposed by the Wriston Committee. I have mentioned this group before, but this time they really outdid themselves. The decree went out that everybody then working for the State Department in Washington either had to resign or join the Foreign Service. Since I had always considered the chancelleries of Europe my natural habitat, I was delighted at this turn of events.

The Foreign Service used to be an elite corps of dedicated, well-educated men who spent two-thirds of their careers abroad manning our embassies and consulates, and the remaining third in Washington running the department for whoever was Secretary of State. I had always admired these returning Foreign Service Officers (FSOs). They had an air of mystery about them, as if they had suffered some unknown disease that somehow set them apart. They all knew each other or about each other, and despite the "perfumed ice pick" with which they sometimes did each other in, they had enormous esprit de corps.

They were, however, outside the mainstream of American life. One story concerns a young FSO who always wore a pin-stripe suit, dark glasses and a bowler hat, and smoked with a long cigarette holder. Even the Foreign Service authorities decided that he had to be rusticated to tone down his appearance, so they assigned him to a month's hard labor in a big filling station outside Dubuque. What happened became something of a legend in the Service. Shortly after the FSO had finished his month at the pumps and was presumably made over into a red-blooded American, it was reported back to the Department that all the attendants at this particular gas station were now wearing bowler hats, dark glasses, and sporting holders when they smoked. The FSO hadn't changed at all.

The old-line Foreign Service hated the Wriston plan which called for "a massive infusion of Main Street" as the only solution to its problem. They fought it tooth and nail, but they couldn't possibly win. After the war the Department had grown so big that it was no longer their own preserve. Representing no constituency "back home," the Foreign Service became a political football and was attacked on all sides as a hopeless anachronism. Its members were known as "cookie pushers"; Joe McCarthy charged that at least ten percent were homosexuals, which proved to be nonsense, but still the damage was done. The former elite corps disintegrated.

I joined the reorganized Foreign Service by way of a process known as "lateral entry." Although this sounds vaguely indecent, it merely meant that you entered the Service at the same salary you were then getting rather than coming in at the bottom of the hierarchy as an FSO-8. In the old days (and, I gather, again today) you had to pass tough written and oral examinations. However, in the first flush of "Wristonization" my examination consisted of virtually nothing more than a man asking me if I ate peas with my knife. I said "No" and there I was, a full-fledged FSO-3.

My first assignment was Antwerp, Belgium, which was not exactly a European chancellery, but it was all very exciting nonetheless. I set off from New York City on the S.S. *United States* armed with one hundred Monte Cristo cigars, a new pair of Head skis and the prospects of a Jaguar XK-140 that I had ordered for delivery in London. I planned a week in England before reporting for duty on the Continent. Diana and the children were to follow later.

An American thinks of England with mixed emotions, much as a child thinks of a divorced mother who was hateful to his father. The English proclivity for regarding us as former colonials doesn't help, nor does their habit of saying they have come "out" to New York or Washington D.C. But, these things having been said, I confess to liking England—and for all the wrong reasons. I enjoy its martial pageantry, its automobiles, its lost empire, and the imprint on good living its upper class has bequeathed us. Then too, although it's not reciprocal, their literature is ours. I tend to skip *Beowulf* and *Gammer Gurton's Needle*, but I go all the way from Shakespeare to P. G. Wodehouse. It was because of the latter's world that I felt the cigars, skis and Jaguar were only the bare essentials.

The English stamp on good living is ubiquitous and readily apparent in almost any corner of what we call the civilized world. Take, for example, clothes. The average Turkoman has his fez and the Frenchman his beret, but as soon as they are ready for the good life (the one frowned upon by President Conant) they retire these bizarre national accoutrements and emerge in what? A Lock hat, suits from Savile Row, shirts from Turnbull and Asser, and shoes by Lobb or Peal. Also, the chances are that they will be driving a Rolls and will pass the port to the left under the watchful eye of the nearest thing to an English butler. The best from other countries never triumphs over the English. The French may have their wines and their haute couture, and the Swiss their paper-thin watches, but like the Chinese who swallow up alien cultures, the upper-class English have absorbed them all in one fine eclectic gobble. Italian paintings, German hock, Russian ballet, you name it—the best from every country is part and parcel of their daily fare—they have made the "good life" theirs.

Let me hasten to say that I would hate to live in England as an Englishman unless I were a peer of ancient lineage, or at least related to one. I know this sounds old-fashioned what with all that's going on in the mod scene today, but I feel that the present fads have nothing like the staying power of the old fad of snobbery. I don't say this with any animosity—some of my best friends are English—but their class consciousness is so ingrained from birth that they can't help themselves, nor do they really want to. I am a snob myself, but when I point out to them that there are more things in heaven and earth than are dreamed of in Debrett, my English friends may agree, but deep inside I know they are thinking, "How very transatlantic."

I have mentioned the English talent for pageantry. Nowhere is this more evident than in their handling of parades. We do very well with the riderless horse bit and the police on motorcycles, but in general our parades have a tendency to fall apart emotionally. A parade, to have any impact, must be seriously martial. The Fife and Drum Corps of Upper Montclair may play and march very well, but they are not associated in the onlooker's mind with any deathdealing unit. A line of drum majorettes prancing and twirling batons is a complete dramatic bust compared with a grizzled bloc of killers like the Ghurkas smartly stepping out to their own outrageous pipes. These small, be-tur-baned Indian troops, each with a wicked knife (*kukri*) in his belt, have a long tradition of fantastic bravery and loyalty to the Crown. One story goes that during some jungle campaign a detachment of Ghurkas was told by their British officer that they would be flown in low at two hundred feet to make their jump. The Ghurkas smiled bravely, but they were definitely not their enthusiastic selves. A sergeant even spoke up refusing to go along with the order— an unprecedented situation. The British officer was dumbfounded, but went on crisply, "You will open your chutes at . . ." Broad grins everywhere. "Ah, parachutes," said the sergeant, "that makes a bit of difference."

Besides parades, the English are very good at lunch. Having made something of a study of the subject myself, I can safely say that lunch as enjoyed in a chic London restaurant by members of the English upper class, or even those aspiring to it, has been raised to the level of a minor art. Money, of course, is no object. Nor is time. What is important is appearance, conversation, and selection. The London lunch is a fruition, a thing in itself, a high point in civilization. Contrast it with our driving executive snatching a sandwich at his desk.

One of the finest little nooks for lunch used to be Wilton's off St. James. There, in cozy elegance, one could order British specialities—smoked salmon from Scotland without a trace of saltiness and a Dover sole fresh from the Channel that morning. With these as a base, one added the touches from other lands that the English are so good at— Scandinavian aquavit, a Moselle from the Rhineland, champagne and brandy from France, Turkish coffee and a fine Havana cigar. The bill was staggering, but settled so to speak, out of court, at a little desk to one side.

While waiting for my car to be delivered, I stayed at the old Cavendish Hotel on Jermyn Street which had been running downhill for some time under the guidance of Edith who had been the head maid in Rosa Lewis's day. The hotel was strong on tea, but weak on water for the tub; the heating and service were almost nonexistent. If you wanted to make a phone call, you had to do it yourself by plugging in the connections at the switchboard. Edith, however, was solicitous about the cold and kept a black fur rug on the floor with which she would cover up the would-be operators. I was sitting so swathed on my second day, hopelessly fiddling with the plugs, when Edith padded back from the front hall. "Your car is here," she said. "Very nice color, too."

It was indeed a thing of beauty—pale apple green with a tan, canvas roof and long sweeping fenders that made it look as though it was doing ninety even when stationary. The chauffeur and I went out for a little spin together around Hyde Park. I let him off at Marble Arch. "It's a pleasure, sir," he said, "to turn over a car like this to a man who knows how to drive." My family, had they been there, would have expected a bolt of lightning to strike him, but then, they think of driving as merely a means of getting safely from A to B.

On approaching Antwerp—I had flown over to the Continent with the car on Silver City Airways—I began to worry about my initial appearance. The head man in Antwerp was Consul General Childs, a long-time FSO, who was said to take a dim view of "Wristonees." I didn't look much like an "infusion of Main Street" but on the other hand, I didn't look the keen young diplomat, either. The skis didn't help a bit. I decided, therefore, to park the car in a garage and report for duty by taxi.

The Antwerp consulate general consisted of about fifty people, a dozen Americans and the rest locals, housed in a new, handsome building of its own on the Avenue de Belgique. The United States Coast Guard maintained a headquarters section on the ground floor, and the United States Treasury had a representative to cover diamond smuggling, but these activities were ancillary to the main purpose of the office, which was twofold.

In 1955, the United States was pursuing a policy of strict limitation on trade with the U.S.S.R. through a vast program known as Export Controls (Ex. Con.). Headed up in the Commerce Department, this program, through the Intelligence community and Foreign Service posts abroad, watched over businesses in the United States, Latin America, and Western Europe that were selling forbidden items to Russia. Antwerp, as the Number 1 transshipment point in East-West trade, was a key spot in the whole operation. As Chief of the "Economic" Section, my job was to report on all such items passing through the port. Once caught by an "economic" report from us, the offending firm in the United States would be had up in Washington and denied all export licenses in the future. If it was not a United States firm, our report would be forwarded to the appropriate government for similar punitive action. The machinery was cumbersome but effective.

The other raison d'etre for a consulate general in Antwerp—only an hour away from the Embassy in Brussels—was the peculiar ethnic division of Belgium between the French-speaking Walloons in the south and the Flemish-speaking Flemings in the north, a situation that required us to have representation in both places. In those days, the Foreign Office and other key departments in Brussels were dominated by the French-speaking element and this was widely resented by the Flemings. Our diplomatic role in Antwerp was to show the flag and make the Flemings feel they were just as important as the Bruxellois. For this we had the round peg in the round hole in the form of our Principal Officer. Prescott Childs and his wife, Roberta, had been in a dozen posts all over the world. They had developed a genuine enjoyment of people and had somehow, at the same time, maintained their iron constitutions. Both qualities were essential for the daily round of lunches, cocktails and dinners to which they were subjected by the Flemish business community.

As Number Two man of the post, I got in on most of these festivities, but in addition, I had to cover the grubbier aspects of Flemish nationalism. The first ceremony I attended in the Stadthuys on the Grand Place in Antwerp was an eye-opener. I had to react visually, because the whole thing was conducted in Flemish and I couldn't understand a word. Drab little men in black crumpled suits would leap from their gilt-backed chairs and become transformed into shaking, passionate figures, as they declaimed interminable poems on the glories of the Flemish past. At that point my only knowledge of the latter was that Elsa von Brabant had been left in the lurch by Lohengrin because she asked too many questions, but that certainly wasn't their problem. At the end a resolution was passed, probably no more than getting a French sign changed somewhere to read in both languages, but the general atmosphere was that of a beer hall putsch. Excessive nationalism anywhere should be made a criminal offense.

I once gave a speech in Flemish, a short one to be sure, but still something of an undertaking. The occasion was a Memorial Day ceremony at the war cemetery in Waregem. My speech consisted of two sentences that I learned by heart from the cook—"I would like to thank the people of Waregem and in particular, the children, for their cooperation on this traditional day."* The second sentence was— "The Reverend Dr. Erwaarde will now give the invocation." That was all—honest, straightforward, simple. Unfortunately, the speech was cut in half by the Reverend Dr. Erwaarde himself who seized the microphone ahead of me

*Ik wens te danken de mensen van Waregem en meestal de kinderen voor hun cooperatie op deze traditionelle dag.

and had already given the invocation before I could introduce him. Nevertheless, as a gesture of goodwill, I think it was much appreciated. The children all waved their flags.

In a gray country like Belgium, flags play an important part enlivening the scene. In almost every little Flemish town with its cobblestones, trolley tracks, and shiny brick villas, there would be some building draped with the red, yellow and black flag of Belgium and, frequently, the lion of Flanders rampant on its field of yellow. Flowers too, planted in solid clumps of color—reds, blues, yellows—did much to *égayer* the municipal greens, which are usually shrouded in mist. The Belgians accept their weather and do everything as if it wasn't raining at all, a tolerable enough approach for golf or shooting, but carried to an extreme when applied to their beach life. Belgians will happily drive to Le Zoute in the pelting rain in order to get the sea air. There's no denying it, they get the sea air, but it leaves something to be desired when they get it by opening the window a crack or by striding along the boardwalk with umbrella, raincoat and hat.

Le Zoute is a night-oriented resort. Underneath the boardwalk there were countless little *boites* for *intime* dancing, or a late snack of onion soup after the Casino. I like casinos, but lamentably these, too, have suffered their infusion of Main Street. The slot machine has completely replaced the Grand Duke, and the result lacks glamour to say the least. No amount of impressive chandeliers can offset a clientele in shorts. Nevertheless in today's Casino one can still pretend to be bilingual in French, which in itself is rather pleasurable. Once one absorbs the fact that *"rien ne va plus"* means no fiddling with the chips, it is quite an easy progression to great idiomatic heights. A good one for a starter is to murmur *"le final sept"* as you languidly push out chips for seven, seventeen, and twenty-seven. To show versatility in the language you can even change to *"le final cinq"* occasionally, but this is rarely done, people being more superstitious at the tables than genuinely culturally oriented. I was stumped for a while by the word *"impairiment,"* which croupiers use all the time as in *"rouge impairiment."* I even looked it up in the dictionary but there was nothing there. Then it came to me one night that the words were *"rouge, impair,* et *manque"* (red, odd, and less than eighteen). These little leaps to knowledge do make life rewarding. As they say, when you stop learning, you stop living.

On those rare days when the sun shines on Le Zoute, the North Sea is still its gray, formidable self pounding against the embankments, but it's then that the café life burgeons. Tables with striped umbrellas spring up everywhere on the boardwalk along with their inevitable concomitants—the handwriting analyst, the one-wheel cyclist, and the itinerant, middle-aged artist who will knock off your girl, or a likeness, with equal facility. It was there, on one of those days when you start drinking at noon and are still chatting at 3:00 A.M., that I learned from some Belgian friends the joys of Amer Picon. Strangely enough, I have never ordered it anywhere else, and it remains enshrined in my taste buds as the epitome of the Belgian seashore.

When one lives in a foreign country for an appreciable length of time, its a very different experience from that of a tourist or visitor. The first impression of Antwerp is appalling, and most tourists, if they get there at all, rush on to Bruges, Brussels or Ghent at the earliest opportunity. The main drag, called Le Meir, runs from the railroad station to the Grand Place and, except for an occasional landmark like the Reubens House, is lined on both sides with shops, cheap eateries and department stores. Its charm is about the equivalent of downtown New Haven, the only difference being that the sidewalk crowds in Antwerp seem to come straight out of Bruegel or Hieronymous Bosch as if there had been no passage of time.

It is on the side streets that Antwerp comes into its own. A few blocks off Le Meir in the heart of town is a *béguinage,* or community of cottages, that serve as almshouses for the destitute. These *béguinages* are named after the Béguines (no connection with Cole Porter), a charitable association of women formed in the twelfth century and formerly widespread throughout Europe. They continue to exist only in the Lowlands. The cottages are immaculate, gay with window boxes, and usually surround a quiet courtyard where the inmates sit in good weather and contemplate their demises.

Near the *béguinage* may be found another feature of Antwerp, namely the discreet small hotel where rooms are let by the hour. The Belgians are an earthy lot; they like to drink, eat, and screw and in about that order. While I daresay these luxurious establishments exist elsewhere (Brussels has several to be sure), I have never seen them in other countries. One can spot a couple lunching in Antwerp and know their destination. Come to think of it, Belgium is a very sexy place with all the appurtenances laid on for dalliance. Again as in Le Zoute, there are countless little *boites* in Antwerp geared to an ambiance that only means one thing. As the wintry winds whip off the Scheldt, these little havens of warmth, some with open fires, but all dark as a pocket with copper and brass plates on the walls, leather chairs, and ancient gleaming wooden bars, provide what man wants most—the almost perfect setting as prelude to the sexual act.

I gravitated to one of these my first night in Belgium and became one of that miserable lot, a lonely man at a bar, than which there is nothing lonelier. The place was called Nostradamus in the shadow of the cathedral and I considered it my spiritual home. There was a three-piece marimba band in one corner, audible but barely visible, since the only illumination came from the lighted shelves of glasses behind the canopied bar. A couple was dancing with abandon on the small square of open carpet between several tables in the middle of the room.

From my point of vantage on the bar stool I could enjoy the girl who was dancing each time she turned to the light. She had a beautiful face flushed with excitement, laughing dark eyes, and gold, hooped earrings. A Flemish gypsy, I thought, as she flung her body around to the beat of the Latin music. Her companion was tall, rather gypsy-looking himself, with a hawklike nose and flashing white teeth. Their group was feeling no pain and soon the others were dancing. One of them, obviously English, had a well-cut coat that lent an air of grace to the dance, although his feet did quite the opposite. Despite the efforts of a willowy blonde to lure him down the Orinoco, his feet maintained a steady Saxon shuffle while he gazed about the room apparently lost in thoughts of his own. Soon a short fellow with a bald head and tufted white hair coming out of his ears, had taken on the Flemish gypsy. His nose, I noted with pleasure, came just to the crevice in her bosom, where it rested, seemingly at peace.

Although I didn't know it at the time, this little group of merrymakers was to become the hard core of our playmates in Antwerp. The music stopped. I paid for my drink and slipped outside to walk back to the hotel. The elderly doorman, resplendent in an Emil Jannings uniform, saluted smartly and insisted on calling me "captain." In no time at all, I learned he was putting his son through MIT. The tip, of course, for so much education could not be that of a deckhand. The old man winked appreciatively and advised me to take in the Lange Nieuw Straat on the way home.

This particular street used to be a feature of Antwerp. One could window-shop for a girl as in Hamburg, but the thing that made Antwerp different was the social gradations of the street. Starting down in the port end of the street, the ladies of the evening hung out of small windows and accosted the passersby. Moving up the scale on the same street, the tenor of the windows changed. By the time you got to the upper end, there was a batch of plate-glass windows much like Saks Fifth Avenue with the ladies sitting behind them attired in evening dress, either reading or sewing, or refinedly sipping coffee. Although the merchandising was fancier, the product was much the same at either end of the street. A year or so before in Antwerp, some outraged Catholic youths had whitewashed all the windows. Before the wash was dry, however, an equally outraged Socialist government had called out the fire department. In no time at all the windows were clean again. The street today I'm sad to report, no longer has these displays. The key-club types have taken over.

At the bottom of the social ladder in Belgium are the Flemish peasants, a gnarled lot in knee-high rubber boots and visored caps who work the same land that their ancestors did in the Middle Ages. Although their life has changed little since then, except for the introduction of bumper pool in all the local cafés, their lands have been rolled over by more wars than any other terrain in history. Towns in Flanders are frequently only one street deep—i.e., a cluster of buildings along the road. If you drive off that main street, you can see the hazy green fields stretching out on either side behind them. These are the polders, dotted with grazing cows and here and there a thatched farm building. Demarcating the big fields are long rows of stumpy trees, willows and pines for the most part, behind which there is usually a barge canal if the trees are running inland. Sometimes on the Ghent-Bruges side of Antwerp, the superstructure of a seagoing vessel will loom up over the trees as a surprising backdrop to the otherwise pastoral scene. Toward the Dutch border, in the area known as the

Campine, such anachronisms are absent.

At the other end of the social scale one sees occasionally in the polders a *water huis*, meaning a house surrounded by a moat. Although some of these are large and impressive, most of them are small chateaux consisting of one or two ancient towers and a permanently lowered drawbridge. Many are still lived in by descendants of the original owners, dating from the days of Charles V and before, people with wonderful names like Pottelsberghe de la Potterie, Brouchoven de Bergeyck, and Pouppez de Kettenis de Hollaeken. Oddly enough, only one of these families has a title. It is a land that proliferates titles, there being no primogeniture in Belgium, and every Count's son is another Count, down to the tenth baby brother. The old Flemish families, however, often have no title at all, a fact on which they pride themselves, secure in their noble quarterings. Four coats of arms, representing the four grandparents, make up into an attractive needlepoint fire screen —eight is better and sixteen better yet, and so forth—but I've never seen one of such simon-pure nobility. Usually some commoner has gotten into the act and thrown the whole thing off, or Aunt Matilda long ago fell prostrate on her needle.

The past is still a big thing in Europe, and nowhere more so than in Belgium. One feels that the occupation of the Lowlands by the Spanish troops of Philip II was only just prior to the occupation by the Germans. The Antwerp Grand Place looks today much as it must have looked in the days of the Duke of Alva. The power and the glory of the Catholic Church as the former unifying force in Europe, can still make itself felt on even a hardened atheist. Most of the time I feel like Mrs. Skewton in *Dombey and Son* when she says, "There is no what's-his-name but Thingummy and what-do-you-call-it is his prophet." And yet . . .

Christmas Eve in Antwerp—snow falling in the port, numbing cold in the Church of St. Paul, and the trumpets blasting in the galleries; the choir soaring, reinforced by a hidden orchestra, and the full force of Catholicism bursting on the individual with the clout of a medieval mace. *Peuple à genoux.* The Cantique de Noel summons the faithful to their knees. It is the ultimate drama.

Following the Midnight Mass, we usually repaired to our friends the Cattles for a traditional supper of oysters on the half-shell, champagne and brown bread thinly sliced and buttered. The Cattles lived well on very little. They were in that nightclub party I witnessed my first night in Antwerp; he was the Englishman and she the Flemish gypsy. Their house, a big one, was a veritable shrine to the culture of the Pays Bas—great ebony mantles over the fireplaces brightened by old Dutch tiles, the walls covered by little-known Dutch and Flemish masters, some very good and the whole a bit run-down. Her mother had been Dutch with at least four coats of arms, and her father had been a judge, *noblesse de robe*, as they say. Both were dead. The house was their only legacy.

Once a year the Cattles would tear the place apart downstairs—three big, high-ceilinged rooms—and give a costume party with a different motif each year. They tend to blur in memory, since the common denominator was alcohol, but one was a South Seas venture with fake palm trees and another was a sailor's joint, with packing crates strewn about and a fish net over the chandeliers. The house now stands gutted by fire, which is not surprising considering its rough usage. In every burnt-out room there are signs in beautifully lettered Gothic script explaining the charred remains. Sometimes the human spirit rises to great heights. There was, of course, no insurance.

Diana and I used to keep a list of friends and acquaintances and after certain names I would put the letter "r"

standing for "robust." By robust I meant not merely vitali-
ty but the ability to enjoy people as they come, with no
prejudgments as to where they fitted in the general scheme
of things. My guiding principle was and is "We are all
companions on the journey to the grave"—a statement
that may have been made by Somerset Maugham, although I've come to think of it as my own. Some find the
idea unpleasant, but to me it merely means that if you look
at the big picture everybody is in the same boat. And that
goes for all races, colors and creeds, rich and poor alike.
The world needs a few shared problems to bring people
together. An invasion from Mars would do it, but the other
is ready to hand.

The trouble is too many people suffer from galloping
xenophobia—i.e., they are not just anti-foreigners but are
against anything foreign to themselves. One group of
friends I know went to the same school, lived together at
college, belonged to the same club, then intermarried and
lived in the same small community, vacationing in winter
on the same small Caribbean Island. They are most unhappy with "outlanders!" On a somewhat larger scale we
saw a similar reaction when, in the founding days of the
United Nations at Dumbarton Oaks, no European would
use the pool if the Chinese delegation had been there first
for their early morning plunge, which was usually the case
because the Chinese swam early to avoid contamination by
the West.

Middle America is peculiarly prone to view with suspicion anything that is foreign. One FSO's wife who came
from the heartland was so anti-foreign that she became a
little legend in her own time. At some post in France she
and her husband took over from their predecessor his house
and his topflight butler. The wife, however, was not about
to be overawed by the latter. When the butler prior to a

dinner party brought up several dusty old bottles of wine from the cellar to the dining room, she turned on him like a fishwife.

"Get those dirty bottles out of here!" she said.

"But Madame," said the butler suavely, "it is customary to *chambrer* the wine."

"I don't care about that," she shouted. "You go chamber them somewhere else!"

European mystiques about drinking are occasionally quite incomprehensible. Wine connoisseurs consider Americans barbaric because of our passion for ice-cold martinis. These, they say, have a ruinous effect on the palate. And yet in Belgium and Holland one is frequently served an ice-cold Dutch gin, Bols or Bokma, and not just one but several. Following these at a gala dinner, after the table wines have been consumed, a hush will fall and the really fine Burgundy will be brought on for delectation in the best glasses. Nobody seems the least worried about their palates having been ruined by the Dutch gin, which is certainly the equivalent of the dry martini. I merely mention this in defense of our own mores which are so often under attack. In what Jefferson called "the vaunted scene of Europe," Americans are generally despised because of our lack of culture and elegance. Patriotically, I did my best to dispel this illusion.

An unlikely promoter of American drinking habits turned up in Antwerp in the form of the Dutch Consul General, Jan vander Mortel, whose cellar in his country house, Huis te Baast, just over the border in Holland was stacked high with bottles of Old Forrester. Jan, a jovial soul, had acquired the taste for bourbon in Chicago where he had been *en poste* for a great many years. One evening after a pheasant shoot at Baast, he decided to expose a mutual friend, Christian de Liedekerke, to a sampling of

his cellar. The effect was glorious to behold. Like a true
European, Christian approached his glass suspiciously,
sipped it gingerly, then, shaking his head appreciatively,
had a little more; finally, wreathed in smiles, he burst out
in enthusiastic endorsement.

Waxing eloquent on the subject of American drinking
and eating habits, we planned an American restaurant in
Paris featuring bourbon on the rocks and the extra dry
martini. This would be no chicken-in-the-rough affair or
hamburger joint, but a really fancy place serving the finest
American dishes, swordfish steak, crabmeat Maryland,
Virginia ham, etc. It might be difficult getting the ingredients but worth the effort in view of the vast market of
continental gourmets who had only been exposed to the
crasser forms of American cookery. We would give them elegance, too. The decor in the bar would be blown-up draw-
ings of Major L'Enfant's plans for Washington. Opening off
this would be the dining room with a scenic wallpaper
showing the surrender of Cornwallis at Yorktown and high-
lighting the all-important French fleet. The place would be
called the Rochambeau, and the whole thing would serve
the higher purpose of binding the two countries together.

Baast was the perfect place for hatching plans of this
sort and doing nothing about them. It was primarily an extremely comfortable, though not luxurious, shooting lodge.
Although once a true *water huis*, it had been done over in
the 1870s along more classical lines and was now a little
jewel of a house with neat whitewashed outbuildings, sitting
on an island formed by the moat and framed in enormous
beeches.

Christian's place in the Ardennes where we also used to
shoot was, on the other hand, an estate. So often one sees
that splendid word "estate" demeaned and truncated
beyond any meaning as in "For Sale: Two-acre estate in
Armonk." An estate has to be large. At its finest, it's

plural. Christian's passed my definition with flying colors —the domain consisted of three or four villages with a population of about six hundred people. There were two chateaux on the property, Noisy and Vêves, the latter having been in the family since the twelfth century. As of our visit, the family lived in one wing of the larger of the two chateaux, a monumental turreted pile of fifty bedrooms built in La Belle Epoque. The rest of the chateau had been turned over to the children of the railroad workers of Belgium who used it for rest and recreation during their vacations. Vêves, the smaller chateau across the valley, has now been restored as an almost perfect example of fifteenth century military architecture. When we were there it was used only occasionally for picnic lunches in the course of a day's shooting.

A shoot at Noisy was a splendid business. The day would start with Christian's father, the old Count, standing on the steps of the chateau and reviewing the beaters who marched by, touching their caps respectfully. It was right out of the Middle Ages, and the beaters might just as well have been pulling their forelocks as tipping their hats. Yet the respect was genuine because Christian's father was also a father to his tenants and had a reputation for helping them, individually and personally, with their problems. After breakfast at a civilized hour, we would draw our numbers and be given a rough sketch showing the geographic layout of the various beats. At this point the head beater, Fernand, who was also the gamekeeper, would always call me Monsieur l'Ambassadeur much to our mutual enjoyment, I because of the easy promotion and he because an ambassador obviously rounded out the quality of the shoot. It used to make Christian uneasy.

The organization was impressive. There would normally be four or five beats in a day, maybe two or three in the morning and two after lunch. Depending on the number of guns, there might be anywhere from twenty to thirty beaters who had to be marshalled into order and started off at the right times. The guns had to be in position at the right time also. The whole thing was synchronized by a mystifying interchange of whistles and hunting horns that never ceased to amaze me. Each hunter drew a number and kept it for the rest of the day. Your only responsibility after that was to find your position on each beat, which was usually designated by a forked stick in the woods with your number on it. Sometimes you would get a good spot and sometimes bad, as the positions were all assigned on a rotating basis. A bad one in my book was a path cut in the woods with only a sliver of open sky above it through which you had to hit the game. You could hear the beaters far off, thrashing through the underbrush as they came closer, then suddenly a whirring noise, a glimpse, a bang and gone. It was surprising, however, how many birds would be shot in situations like this.

There was a friend of Christian's father, a crack shot, in just such a spot down the line from me one day. I was fascinated because here we were deep in the woods and the older gentleman had his man waiting on him hand and foot. The man opened up the shooting seat, then a small portable table on which he placed a wine glass after duly polishing it with a napkin. The Vicomte de —— sat down with his gun between his legs and his man proceeded to pour a little wine in the glass. The Vicomte tasted it and put it down. Suddenly there was that whirring noise, a bang, and a big cock pheasant plummeted into the alley between us. The Vicomte sat down again and his man finished filling up his glass. I learned later that the Vicomte had fought gallantly in the last war until his man had been wounded, at which point he decided to withdraw from all further engagements which he apparently did with impunity.

Dinners at Noisy were always formal, with handwritten cards on little silver stands listing the courses to come. Usually the *pièce de résistance* would be a specialty of the countryside which, beside pheasant and woodcock, included hare and at times wild boar. The wines and the guests came from Paris. The latter invariably spoke fluent English. After dinner there would be one or two tables of bridge in the library and another group talking around the fireplace. The library was a huge room lined with beautiful leather-bound books that took up three of the walls. It was the central room of the family's wing.

One night in the talking group I suggested as a diversion that we each write down quickly off the top of our heads a short list of our basic reading about the other fellow's country. It is a simple game; any number can play, providing you have two nationalities represented, and it frequently turns up one or two oddities. Witness below:

My List on France	*The French List on the U.S.*
Molière Plays	De Toqueville's America
Quentin Durward	Gone With the Wind
The Three Musketeers	Collected Works of Horatio Alger!
A Tale of Two Cities	
Madame Bovary	
Tartarin de Tarascon	

Much to my surprise the French had never read *A Tale of Two Cities* and, somewhat to theirs, I pointed out that Alger was not considered a really topflight author. The English, for their part, have all read *GWTW* and possibly *Huckleberry Finn*, but that's about the extent of their reading on America. How can the U.N. hope to get off the ground when the so-called elite of each country are familiar with such a thin veneer of the literature of the other. I feel that somewhere in here a trained cultural psychologist, if there is such a "discipline," could work up a neat little something.

One night in Paris I ran afoul of my daughter Daphne's innate nationalism. A father is normally proud of his daughter but that night she was an absolute lump. Possibly it was her age, which was only sixteen. We had taken her to a gala charity ball at the Chateau de Groussay, which was one of those long, low buildings vaguely reminiscent of Fontainebleau. As we drove up in our rented Citroen, I felt we should have been in a Dufy landau behind a pair of bays with two men on the box. Candles lit all the windows and footmen in powdered wigs and yellow sateen britches made the whole thing look like a scene from *Die Fledermaus*. Daphne, I thought, seemed to brighten momentarily, but I was wrong. She had flown over from school the day before and her bags had gone to Zurich. Faced with the crisis, Diana had solved the problem by having her turned over to a Mme. Spanier in Balmain to act as a model for one of the house's creations—a light blue number called "sea foam" made of hundreds of starched ruffles. Daphne, after moodily staring in the mirror, said she looked like a bloated Tinker Bell. This frame of mind seemed to have settled permanently. "I hate the French," she said.

The chateau was all glitter. There was an *intime* play produced in the private theater, a rococo jewel of a room, followed by dancing and a champagne supper of pate de foie gras and ortolans à la Brissac. *Tout* Paris was there, countless vicomtesses, the Duke and Duchess of Windsor, and Mme. A. Onassis (an earlier version than Jackie). In fact, everybody was in such a tizzy looking at each other that a splendid midnight snack must have been eaten afterwards by the powdered footmen offstage. Our friends, the Liedekerkes, had produced a young Duc for Daphne's benefit, but it was all to no avail. The French think very highly of Ducs, but as far as she was concerned he was just an odd little foreigner. My beautiful daughter refused to dance and never opened her mouth. The Duc spoke perfect English so there wasn't a language barrier.

I had to take her for a walk in the gardens. After a short stroll we discovered a deserted pavilion where we settled ourselves on a settee between tubbed orange trees and, for the first time since her arrival, she relaxed. Occasionally, strolling members of the *haut monde* would look in on us and bow politely, always with a knowing smile. Obviously in their eyes Tinker Bell was La Belle Otero. We held a happy court, graciously nodding back. I felt a glow of parental pride. "You are growing up," I said.

The last three months of my continental tour were spent at the State Department's French language school in Nice. My recollections are that it was a well-meaning endeavor but essentially a giant boondoggle that would be consumed by the wrath of Congressman Rooney of the Appropriations Committee, which is what eventually happened. Somewhere along the line the Department had bought an enormous villa in Nice which it felt constrained to make use of and so had drafted from various posts abroad a motley assortment of personnel. Some were bright young men with a flair for language, and I think it helped them, but the majority were clods. No amount of instruction could ever transform them into linguists.

We had two pretty teachers, one the wife of the conductor of the local symphony and the other the wife of the heir apparent to the Lanson Champagne Company. After class one day I took one of them for a swim in the azure blue Mediterranean, which from the villa's terrace looked just the way it does in a travel poster. The villa was in the hills back of Nice. As we drove down nearer the shore, I noticed what looked like a fairly wide band of driftwood in the water lapping the beach. It began to dawn on me that this band was not driftwood at all but, in fact, a most unromantic substance, the product of a thousand drains. Nothing daunted, my companion laughed happily and grabbing a rubber mattress from a pile on the beach motioned me to do the same. *"Un moment . . . C'est finis."* We both paddled manfully and in *un moment* it was true, we were out beyond the band of brown and lazing in the azure blue. I suppose the moral of this little story is—you can put up with an awful lot of crap if you think what you're doing is worthwhile. She was a lovely girl.

At the end of the course, presumably honed to perfection in French, I returned to Antwerp to find that the Department in its wisdom had assigned me to Aruba in the Dutch West Indies. They speak Dutch, Spanish, and a local dialect known as papiamento in Aruba, but certainly not a word of French. I thought there must be some mistake, but there were the orders in front of me. When it comes time to move on, one makes a mental list of posts where one might conceivably be sent. Aruba wasn't on my list. I had to look it up on the map. Just off the coast of Venezuela. I can't say that I was overjoyed. Still, looking on the bright side, it would be my own post. If you go in for that type of thing, there's something to be said for being head man, even if it's on a lesser Antille.

On home leave from Belgium that summer we paid a visit to Father in Lawrence. He had just returned from a trip to Maine where he had painfully twisted his ankle walking up Mt. Desert. I was shocked by how he had aged in the last two years. At his suggestion I went into New York for a review of his financial affairs with his lawyer. The next day, the last of our short visit, it was obvious that he wanted me to praise him for what he had built up by way of a fortune during his lifetime. He was sitting in a chair, looking very feeble, with his leg up on an ottoman, but for some reason I couldn't bring myself to do it. I kept saying, "Yes, they showed me everything," but that extra little praise that he wanted to hear just wouldn't come out. It was too great a reversal of roles. I shook his hand and said goodbye, then left the room. I came back a moment later and placed my hand on his shoulder. Still no words, but we smiled. It was the last time I saw him. He died a month later after our return to Belgium. The New York funeral was a stiff-upperlip affair in the full panoply of the Episcopal Church, Dr. Arthur Kinsolving presiding. After the ceremony I got drunk. In a strange way Father and I had been close.

CHAPTER

My Foreign Service "game plan," if you could dignify it by such a term, originally envisioned two or three Western European posts as Consul or First Secretary (the Consular and Diplomatic Services are interchangeable under the Foreign Service Act of 1924), eventually ending up as a Consul General in the Caribbean area. Not taxing exactly, but a reputable and presumably interesting career.

Consul Generaling is the cheap way to become an Ambassador. You get a brace of flags on your car, a chauffeur, gilt-edged china with the seal of the United States in the center, even brandy snifters with the same seal, an entertainment allowance, and a well-furnished house—and none of it costs you a penny. Furthermore, if you are sufficiently removed from any supervising embassy, you are, in effect, totally independent, reporting directly to the Department of State. I highly recommend it to any young person who enjoys the furbelows of living.

I had contemplated, however, a further sampling of the Continent before enjoying my just rewards in the above manner. But this apparently was not to be. There I was, serving the country in a small way by demonstrating to an incredulous coterie of Europeans that all Americans were not like our prototype, when I was cut off in my prime and shipped where? Not Paris, Rome or Madrid—but Aruba, a place I'd never even heard of.

Somebody may have thought I was a playboy and decided to take steps to remove me from the Western world. All
organizations have their Cesare Borgia types lurking behind the everyday exteriors. I think it more likely, though,
that I was simply a body due for reassignment and there
was this slot to be filled in the Dutch West Indies. The fact
that I had barely gotten my feet wet in the European
trough was of concern to nobody but me.

Aruba is a sixty-eight-square-mile island at the bottom
end of the Caribbean which together with Bonaire, Cura-
cao and the Dutch Windward Islands to the north makes
up the Netherlands Antilles Government, an equal partner
along with Holland in the Kingdom of the Netherlands.
United States representation on Aruba commenced in 1942
after the arrival of American forces during the war. Primarily the consulate served the Lago Oil Company, a sub-
sidiary of Standard Oil, whose giant refinery complex and
living quarters took up the whole southeastern end of the
island. Crude oil came in tankers from Maracaibo on the
Venezuelan coast only twenty-five miles to the south and
was processed by the Lago refinery which, after Abadan in
Iran, was meant to be the largest operating refinery in the
world. At least that was what I was told by the Esso people. I didn't argue. Shell had a similar operation on Cura-
cao which looked every bit as big. At night sometimes, I
would look nostalgically at the lights on the refinery flume
pipes and funnels which in the distance gave the effect of a
giant block of apartment buildings, rather like Central
Park South in New York City—very pleasing until the
mind's eye saw that the whole contraption was just little
catwalks in the sky connecting the lights together.

The Lago colony used to consist of some three thousand
permanent American expatriates, but by 1960 this figure
had been cut in half. Nevertheless Lago was virtually a
principality of its own. The ruling prince, a short, stocky

man named Odis Menzies (pronounced Mingus) had been there since its inception. He presided over the births, deaths, marriages, and divorces of his subjects with Olympian justice and concern. His house was the finest in the compound, complete with a swimming pool at a time when pools were rare. It sat high on a promontory looking out to sea through luxuriant imported planting. His wines and food were also imported and prepared by his own French chef. He knew every last child in the colony and lived simply, albeit in the style of an absolute monarch, which he was.

Lago society was rigid. Engineers went out with other engineers, managers entertained other managers, but never could a manager have an engineer for dinner, or vice versa. I don't know whether this divide-and-rule approach was company or Menzies policy; it simply wasn't done. We were pigeonholed in the managerial group, which was all right by me as I am not very good with engineers.

Fortunately, by the time we got to Aruba, the consulate had been moved out of the Lago compound to Oranjestad, the provincial capital, so one felt less like an employee of Esso. Oranjestad boasted a thriving shopping street for cut-rate cameras, watches, perfumes, and so forth. It had its own harbor for the cruise-boat trade. It was situated halfway between Lago and the western end of the island, where an elaborate Casino Hotel had just been built. Connecting the hotel, Oranjestad and Lago at that time was a two-lane highway about eighteen miles long. It ran through the Kunuku, the local name for the desolate countryside of volcanic rock and brush where the only signs of life were an occasional rooting goat and a streaming strip of toilet paper impaled on a cactus hedge.

The youngish but graying Lago lieutenants (managers) met us in the cocktail lounge of the Grace Line's *Santa Rosa*. Diana was with me looking like Gatsby's Daisy in a white floppy hat, green and white blouse, and white pleated skirt. My own gray flannel pinstripe and Union Club tie were impeccable. The Lago lieutenants seemed pleased. I overheard them by chance in the washroom after three or four martinis: "Well," said one, "the State Department's done us proud this time." "Yup," said the other, "not the bottom of the barrel." Now admittedly both were in their cups, and the praise was somewhat tempered, but I wondered if just being what I was might not have a certain value. I had begun to realize in Washington that the WASP gentleman was held in some esteem as he also was on Belgian "shoots," but these were snobbish situations. In Aruba I learned that ordinary Americans abroad put a premium on the category. I hoped to live up to their expectations.

We had not been in Aruba more than a month, however, before it seemed clear to me that the post should be abolished. There was a perfectly good consulate general in Curaçao which was only forty minutes away by air and could handle any and all Aruban problems. The only reason we still maintained a consulate on Aruba was to butter up Esso's ego. Even Lago didn't care much any more. Arubans sneer at the Curaçaloñs because the latter have Negro blood whereas the native Aruban is a "pure" mixture of Indian, Dutch and Spanish. Again scarcely a valid reason for maintaining a separate office. Culturally, the Arubans were divided into two camps—the vast majority who favored Louis Armstrong, and a small, struggling group of would-be intellectuals who patronized concerts by wandering harpists, oboe players and the like. The latter group revolved around the Aruban Cultural Center, which was more than pleased with any cultural program the United States dangled before it. The value to the center was undeniable; to the United States, to put it kindly, it was debatable.

One could get pious, too, about the cost of the consulate to the taxpayer. This was not great as bureaucratic wastage goes, but annual running expenses were over $75,000 which, in addition to a dollar investment in Aruba for the Principal Officer's "residence" ($36,000 purchase price in 1948 and some $5,000 worth of furniture), made a grand total of $116,000—and for absolutely nothing of value to the United States in return.

One incidental expense that always fascinated me was the ordering of a new flag for the residence every two months. There was a tall flagpole in the front garden, and the flag was always flat out in the wind. After sixty days "Old Glory" became a square, the end of the stripes having frayed away. I suppose, if left to its own devices, the flag would have whittled itself down to the field of stars and eventually down to the pole itself. This occurrence would have been most unseemly so it was changed as soon as it got square.

We stayed in Aruba through three flags. I had written a detailed memorandum to the Department recommending closing of the post, which apparently coincided with their own thinking. Had I but known all this was going on at home, I would have felt considerably better. One glorious day, the phone rang and it was Washington. The voice at the other end said that they were moving me further north.

"May I ask where?"

"Nassau," said the voice. My heart leapt—the Bahamas, civilization, "Hig Leaf" (High Life) as the Belgians say, and a nice consul generalship! "We feel you'll be a round peg in a round hole."

"I will certainly attempt to comply," I said, sinking back in my chair.

Diana took the good news somewhat more calmly than I did. Obviously she didn't want to spend any more time on Aruba than was necessary and thought Nassau would be a great improvement, but she pointed out that the past six months had not been all that bad. I have been a little harsh on Aruba; it did have certain bizarre charms and entertainments, like watching the sharks feed on the refuse from the abattoir. This little drama took place in a small bay on the north side of the island and involved a scenic drive through the previously mentioned Kunuku.

I knew what she meant, however. Unless they are hopelessly dependent on one another, most couples over the years are subject to cracks in their solid-state circuitry. Under the impact of the "good life" in Europe, Diana and I had somewhat drifted apart. Adversity now had brought us closer together than we had been for some time. Aruba, of course, was not adversity at all, except in terms of pride and a sense of isolation. Nevertheless, the clandestine lunch was now a thing of the past, and we were both thrown back on our own resources to cultivate our garden. In some circles I believe this is known as straightening up and flying right. Strangely enough, it brings its own rewards.

Diana is actually an enthusiastic gardener and soon made our patio into a thing of beauty with a small waterfall and a variegated selection of crotons—that multicolored leafy plant that thrives in the equatorial sun. I bought a Japanese telescope which when focused on Jupiter revealed four of its thirteen moons, the four discovered by Galileo. To the layman these moons are very satisfactory because of their speedy orbit around the planet. You could be having cocktails before dinner and all four moons would be lined up on the right side of Jupiter. Coming back after dinner for coffee, the moons would be split— two on the right and two on the left. A little later it would be three on the left, and eventually, depending on when you went to bed, all four would have changed sides.

I found it rather soothing to think of all this apparently

senseless activity going on up there day in and day out. Here was something fixed you could count on in this changing world. On our quiet evenings at home, of which there were quite a few, we often used to play Bernstein's version of *Candide* on the phonograph. I doubt if this really qualifies as proper "music of the spheres," but at the time it seemed to us the perfect accompaniment for those poor frenetic moons.

Aruba had other benefits besides this rather odd resuscitation of home life. The beaches on the south shore are superb. If nothing else, I'm a connoisseur on the feel of sand on the balls of my feet. Aruba's couldn't be softer or finer. Also, in Aruba you can be absolutely sure of sun every day of your winter vacation. In addition, there was an excellent Indonesian restaurant in the harbor of Oranjestad where they served a good *rijstaffel* and another Dutch dish consisting of thick juicy steak with a fried egg on top. The barge was moored to the dock; you ate inside in a cozy, dimity-curtained atmosphere, but there were also a few tables dockside for coffee. Sitting there after dinner in the evening when the wind dropped, the harbor could be beautifully still. One of the Grace Line's *Santa* ships would be sitting in the roads like a jewel, while the more primitive lanterns of the fishing boats at the dock cast shadows on the colonnade of a Dutch colonial customs shed that ran the length of the quai.

In the name of progress the colonial building was scheduled for early demolition to make way for a supermarket. In my one attempt to do something for Aruba I begged with the authorities to save it. People on cruise boats, I pointed out, pay thousands of dollars and come thousands of miles to get away from supermarkets. What they want to see is that old building, not the same thing they've left behind them. But as authorities go, the Dutch are probably the most inflexible, and nothing was going to move them. The night we departed from Aruba the building was still standing, but it was definitely doomed.

That night was an odd one. All the bags and other impedimenta had been shipped to the *Santa Paula* during the day, so all we had to do was walk on board when we felt like it. As the ship didn't sail until 3 A.M. this left a pleasant evening interlude before embarking.

The evening started with a blessing by the maids. Domestic service in Aruba is unusual—frequently a female cook and a maid will be "married," that is to say they live together when unemployed and hire out as a couple when working. Ours were a dour, taciturn pair. The maid, when berated by Diana one day for not responding to her cheery good morning, replied, "I can't help it ma'am, I'se just naturally sour." It came as some surprise then, as we got in the car to drive to a farewell dinner at the hotel, to see the two of them standing in the driveway, weeping and waving and making signs of the cross. This is a hard thing to play along with. You can't really roll down the window and shout out, "I didn't know you cared." I settled for blowing kisses as if I was running for office. Diana felt I rather overdid it considering I couldn't tell them apart.

The other strange thing that night was my luck at the casino. I simply could not lose at blackjack. Time and again I would be dealt a pair of aces which I split, putting both face up on the table and doubling the bet. Inevitably the next card dealt to each would be a face card, making the magic twenty-one and paying off two and a half to one. If not the aces, I'd get some other combination, always perfect in relation to the dealer. It was fantastic. A tiny crowd gathered to watch. Starting with twenty dollars, I parlayed things along to four hundred dollars, at which delightful figure I quit as it was time to leave for the boat.

One always wonders about casinos. I had the definite feeling with this one that they were giving me a farewell present so that I would go away with a nice warm feeling and say what a great place it was. Who knows? The cards come out of that shoe box so apparently at random. Cognoscenti of the tables say that the time to watch for any man-made adjustment of this random order is when a new dealer relieves his colleague. The new dealer with a palmed card can easily make it appear to be coming out of the shoe. But this is a limited effort at best and is usually reserved for drunken high bettors. If the trend is with you, you can't fail.

It was not kind to Aruba, but before departure I couldn't resist mailing out to friends a mimeographed card which read as follows:

> *Mr. & Mrs. J. Lawrence Barnard*
> *announce with pleasure*
> *a change of address to*
> *The American Consulate General*
> *Nassau, Bahamas*

My first impression of Nassau was of the greenness of the island and its trees—palms, of course, but a variety of others, tall casuarina pines, poincianas, beach plums, sea grapes, and grass (not just on people's lawns, but public grass). The water truthfully was advertised: crystal clear and sky blue over the white-sand shallows, then ultramarine in the deep sea beyond the coral reefs that lined the island. The reefs were sometimes clearly defined by a long, curling line of white foam. When this happens the Bahamians call it a "rage on the reef." It's a great phrase, but I prefer the line "Oh sweet it is in Aves to listen to the roar/of the breakers on the reef outside that never touch the shore."

We took over a house called West Lea outside of town on Cable Beach which had been occupied by the previous

Consul General. The United States Government didn't own the house, we rented it on our own and were reimbursed. It was a good house with kitchen, dining room and a small study downstairs and four bedrooms and a huge living room upstairs. Opening off the living room was a wide-screened porch with an uninterrupted view of the sea. Just under the living room, the dining room opened on a garden distinguished by Victorian female statues representing the four seasons. To the right of the drive and well-protected by a thick, well-groomed casuarina hedge was an enormous swimming pool, very handsome, but seemingly in need of repair as its color was an opaque green.

Happily, other than the moribund pool, there was very little fixing-up that needed to be done. The house was expensively furnished as the government had previously owned a house in town that was considered a showpiece, and the furniture from it had been transferred to ours in toto. We concentrated on putting in a brilliant green carpet on the staircase in the front hall and some heavy long white curtains on the stair landing. They gave the entrance a *faites vos jeux* atmosphere that instinctively led one upstairs. I don't want to imply that we ran a gambling joint—we rarely played anything but bridge at a tenth—I just want to point out that the house was a natural for entertaining.

I must admit I love to entertain. The part I like best is that pause before anyone comes. You have just emerged clean and neat from a bath in your best bib and tucker. The stage is set, everything is as attractive as you can make it—fresh flowers, ice, canapés, shining glasses, liquor, all ready for the onslaught. It's a great moment and the butler says softly from behind the bar, "Can I fix you something, Mr. Barnard?" A very light vodka and tonic, of course, is the only reply at this juncture. One can't be doing a little jig in the hallway as the first guests arrive.

Nassau—by the pool

Diana doesn't take to this moment the way I do. She has a tendency to look at her watch and wonder if anyone is coming at all.

Our first official cocktail party was very official indeed. We had, amongst others, the then Premier, Sir Roland Symonette and his wife, Lady Symonette, the Chief Justice, the Attorney General, the Solicitor General, and the Receiver General. The last three gentlemen came together in a batch, and I was reminded of the time in Washington when Messrs. Frankfurter, Hamburger, Swett, and Clapp crossed our portal in that order. As Consul General, it seemed to me that the other three "Generals" and I should form some kind of a club—nothing specific of course, a coffee klatch perhaps—but I didn't push it. At first encounter with our British cousins, particularly the colonial variety, it's best to be noncommittal.

There were already one or two raised eyebrows among the stuffier wives because of one of my guests. I had asked our black receptionist at the office, Brenda Major, who was about to win the title of Miss Bahamas in the first Bahamian beauty contest. Brenda came, looked like the knockout that she was, and had a marvelous time (I kept a fatherly eye on her). When it came time to leave, she shook my hand, laughing but earnest. "Thank you," she said. "Thank you for having a real Bahamian."

She had a point. My list consisted primarily of British colonial officials and representatives of the white merchant minority, the so-called Bay Street Boys who were then firmly in control of the politics and economy of the Islands. This white minority, of course, were real Bahamians, too, having lived there for generations. Some were descended from the Eleutherian Adventurers, Puritan dissenters who came down from Bermuda in the mid-seventeenth century. All of them had a fierce pride in the Bahamas, which they tended to regard as their own private fiefdom. The population of the Islands, however, was then over eight-six percent black, a fact that lent a certain validity to Brenda's parting words.

The black-white problem as far as the blacks are concerned has now been resolved satisfactorily in the Bahamas. The Union Jack has come down, replaced by a handsome new Bahamian flag—black, golden yellow and aquamarine blue. The Bay Street Boys have been routed politically, there is a black Governor-General and Prime Minister, and the independent Government of the Bahamas is a member of the U.N.

In the process of accomplishing all this there was, as expected, minor trouble: demonstrations on Bay Street, wild talk of invasions by Castro, and rumors of armed uprisings. The mace, the symbol of British rule, was thrown out the window of Parliament by the leader of the opposition— much to the enjoyment of all the demonstrators on Bay Street and to the horror of our normal cocktail guests. I had been tipped off that something was going to happen, so, armed with binoculars, I had an eyewitness view from my office window of the whole affair. The mace was quickly followed by a smaller object thrown out by the present Governor-General. I discovered later that it was the hourglass with which the Speaker of the House used to curtail his speeches! The British garrison had been reinforced, several frigates lay offshore, but not a single shot was fired on either side nor were there any casualties whatever.

How did the Bahamas move out of their colonial status in such a quiet revolution? The answer probably lies in the fact that the British considered the Bahamas more of a headache than a jewel in the crown of Empire and were glad to be rid of them. The white Bay Street Boy's first loyalty was to their Bahamas, not England. Charges of their selling out to the Mafia made excellent propaganda, but primarily their downfall lay in the reapportionment of seats in the House of Assembly. The island of New Providence on which Nassau is situated is overwhelmingly the most populous and has long been a stronghold of the black opposition. The power of the Bay Street Boys depended on their safe constituencies in the backward Out Islands which for years had allowed them to control nineteen out of a total of thirty-three parliamentary seats with only thirty-six percent of the popular vote, while the Progressive Liberal Party with forty-four percent of the popular vote had only eight seats. Obviously this situation had to change.

People ask me about the Bahamas today. Around New York one gets the impression from the questions asked that you're taking your life in your hands to go there at all. I must say that the spate of racist murders in St. Croix and the shooting of the Governor in Bermuda have a tendency to cool one's ardor for a winter vacation on any "Island in the Sun." The stupidest way for an individual to end his days is by getting shot because of his color or nationality. Yet innocent people all over the "civilized" world are getting knifed or shot for these reasons. Although it's not a fair comparison because of numbers and crowding, compared to New York City, Nassau is a paragon of racial harmony. I once took Bob Wagner, New York's ex-Mayor, for a courtesy call on the local Governor who, in the course of the conversation, mentioned that the black population of the Bahamas was 160,000. Wagner smiled slightly when asked how many blacks there were in New York City. "Add one and a half million," he said. There is a radical wing within the ruling party in Nassau, but at present this wing is more than counterbalanced by a rising middle class of blacks who have a vested interest in law and order. The current leaders, many of them London-trained lawyers, have been described as Afro-Saxons. They wear striped trousers and top hats rather than dashikis on ceremonial occasions. The term is not widespread, but it is useful for distinguishing them from the more radical element.

The Nassau black leaders have been truly progressive (witness their accomplishments). They are totally committed to raising the dignity of their people who, in the words of the current premier, Lynden Pindling, have long been "subject to many forms of degradation, from the downright beastliness of slavery to the more economic and social indignities of inequality." Their main problem is that the local schools are exploding with tiny tots, and some not so tiny standing on street corners, all with rising expectations that a one-industry economy like the Bahamas simply cannot satisfy.

The one industry is tourism and its offshoots. The Bahamians grow onions in the Exumas and tomatoes and the sweetest pineapples in the world on Eleuthera, but none of these in sufficient quantity to be a major export. They have salt in Inagua and Long Island. There is a cement plant and a refinery (and another in the planning stages) on Grand Bahama; they have low-cost housing projects on New Providence; and they have a monopoly on the aragonite needed in the manufacture of cement and glass, which ingredient is sucked from the ocean floor near Bimini. In the absence of tourism, however, none of these can be expected to provide enough employment to keep pace with the soaring birthrate. All those tiny tots cannot go back to the Out Islands and live off peas and rice, and they cannot all go to the United States. Although the Bahamian government may not want to raise generations of busboys, that is what they are facing unless a miracle (or a debacle) occurs. Immediately following independence, hotel staffs and taxi drivers displayed a notable surliness toward tourists. To preserve this essential business, the government instigated a "politeness" campaign which has had considerable success, and now, fortunately, the problem seems more in hand. There is always the off chance, of course, that some street-corner gang in Nassau, crazed on drugs, will drive to Lyford Cay and shoot up some of the Beautiful People—but that could happen anywhere.

The Bahamas have had their revolution and Nassau today is probably the most tranquil tourist paradise in the Caribbean. Prime Minister Pindling came to power with a messianic mission "to throw the (white) rascals out." Some might say today he has merely changed the color of the rascals. Mr. Pindling is now more of a political moderate than when he started, a fact which infuriates the left wing of his party, many of whom feel he has sold out the party's ideals. Faced with the necessity of appeasing them, he occasionally makes a speech about redistributing the wealth, but of the two choices facing a developing country—socialism or capitalism—he is definitely committed to the latter, primarily because the Bahamas is so completely geared to the United States economy and its attendant value system. Only a megalomaniacal monk like Savonarola destroys the Golden Goose, and Mr. Pindling doesn't fit the role. Known as "Little Moses," he has a large popular following that looks upon him as the symbol of their new-found national pride. To be sure, his present way of life is a far cry from the bullrushes of his namesake. Mrs. Pindling is the epitome of chic and should appear permanently on the cover of *Ebony*. His house and grounds, Rolls Royce and yacht, bespeak a man who enjoys material well-being. Although his own back-benchers complain about him bitterly, the rank and file of his party don't begrudge him what he has because it's what they all want themselves. His constituents gave him the Rolls!

Charges that the present government is a corrupt, insolvent dictatorship are made by the opposition—essentially a middle-class party made up of Pindling dissidents and former "Bay Street" elements. Many have a high IQ, but few have the common touch. Although the treasury is in a parlous state, unless the economic situation takes a sudden turn for the worse, Mr. Pindling's charisma is likely to carry him through. His own left wing at the moment has no viable candidates to put forward; neither does the opposition. Also in his favor is the fact that the Bahamas actually benefit from a United States recession since American tourists tend to forego Europe for shorter, less expensive trips. Should tourism dry up completely, the Bahamas are in for a bad time. The Bahamians are humorous, easygoing people—scarcely the "cool, calculating killing machines" desired by Eldridge Cleaver. But under stress, or a decade from now, who knows? Mammon has had a long record of worship in the "Isles of June," but if times get really tough a Savonarola type might well be in the cards.

These jagged rocks below the ice were virtually invisible when we first came to Nassau in 1960. Government House shone in all its glory. Its dinner invitations had gilt edges and the ladies wore long white gloves (they still do), and they didn't smoke before the toast to the Queen (they still don't). After the ladies had departed the gentlemen lingered over the port and cigars in the dining room. One memorable evening at Government House I brought a high-ranking American admiral as a guest. I had the car with all flags flying drive out on the tarmac at the airport to meet his personal plane that afternoon, and we drove to West Lea for a drink before he went on to his hotel to change for dinner. This was my first exposure to a top-level admiral and I was much impressed by his entourage—a lesser admiral, several captains and two ADCs who were constantly leaping up with their cigarette lighters at the ready. The admiral himself was a feisty little man emblazoned in ribbons, about four rows, and reputed to be very, very bright. He had two bourbon on the rocks. I picked him up at the hotel about an hour later, and he, Diana and I drove to Government House. During the cocktail period the

Admiral had two more whiskies, unfortunately not bourbon as the English don't recognize our native product. It might have been this shift over to the more traditional whiskey that unloosed the Admiral's tongue after dinner, but I rather suspect it was one or two bourbons taken at his hotel during the changing period. In any case, there we were at the cleared and polished table over the port and cigars when I heard to my horror the Admiral's voice ringing out, "The trouble with the British is they're no damn good. They won't fight." I don't know what the subject matter was, he had been talking to the Governor's ADC—a mild-mannered little man whose main interests in life were his clothes, his clubs and racing. He must have gotten out beyond his depth. The effect, however, was electrifying. The Governor, a tall man, stiffened in his chair. "Shall we go outside?" he said. The Admiral must have thought he was in for a donnybrook because he looked over at me for support. "We go out and water the flowers," I said. It was a personal wrinkle to tradition added by the then Governor. I picked out a nice hibiscus next to His Excellency. "All those ribbons," I whispered, "but not one of them for tact." The Governor, who was having some difficulty getting started, smiled frostily, then went about the business at hand. It was the height of my diplomatic career.

We had a lot of Navy visits. For the most part these went off very well. The ships and their crews came in for rest and relaxation, and the latter was always efficiently handled by the Navy's Shore Patrol. The procedure was that if the ship was commanded by a captain or less, he paid a courtesy call on me and then I returned the courtesy by calling on him. If the commanding officer was higher in rank than a captain, I paid the first call. Only once did we have an impasse and that was when a ship came in commanded by a captain who had just been named admiral-designate. Neither of us budged.

The first call I made on one of our destroyers almost ended in disgrace. A consul general is piped on board with everybody standing at attention. After an exchange of salutes and handshaking, he is led off to the commanding officer's cabin. Not so on the way out. After he has made his farewell, he is pretty much on his own. The rule book says he must face the quarter deck and give the civilian salute with his hat held over his left breast. The book doesn't go on. Meanwhile the honor guard is at present arms and the bosun's mate is piping away. As a novice at this kind of thing, it seemed to me only polite to stand on the gangplank until the piper had finished his musical endeavor. It was only after I noticed the notes growing fainter and a few sidelong glances in the honor guard that I gathered I was meant to have left. If the piper had fallen flat on his face, I suppose I would have left sooner.

It is abundantly clear by now that my relations with the great have been tangential to say the most. Never was this more apparent than in my relations with Richard Nixon, who slipped into Nassau just after he lost the election to Kennedy. Years ago he dropped in on us one evening in Georgetown in the company of a friend, Don Jackson. They had both come from a Republican Marching-and-Chowder Club dinner. Our own group was having a fine time, but Mr. Nixon seemed disinclined to mingle. (He could have been either shy or showing disapproval of the effete East.) Instead, he sat down alone at an upright piano we had in the hall and played it ruminatively, lost in thoughts of his own. After a while, when I realized the music had stopped, I went out in the hall to freshen his drink, but he had gone. In Nassau, he was even more uncommunicative. Granted he was suffering from one of his defeats, but as Consul General I had left a note for him at the Balmoral Club, saying that the Governor would very much like to talk to him and asking him to call me. I could express his regrets if he wanted. After all, he was still Vice-President. There was no reaction whatever. Owing to a tip by a friend, Bob Lee, who was also staying at the Balmoral, I caught up with him at the airport when he was leaving. We shook hands earnestly while we were photographed. "Aw, I'm on vacation," he said when I asked if he had gotten my note. As he turned away to step on the plane, I found I was holding a golf ball inscribed with his name. It was almost sleight of hand.

In a well run consulate general, visas, passports and citizenship matters are handled by the staff. I was blessed with an extremely capable number-two in the person of Consul Olive Jensen, who headed up a staff of four Americans and twelve locals. Olive handled with great efficiency all routine office business, keeping me in reserve as a court of appeal. This left me free to indulge in such higher realms of thought as political and economic reporting and the sometimes arduous task of representing the country. The latter is a full-time job, not just a nine to five one.

There are two schools of thought on representation. Congressman Rooney always maintained that our foreign emissaries should be representative of the United States and live as such, that is, a typical Joe in a bungalow with a rumpus room in the basement. He voted funds accordingly. The other school (mine) believes that the principal officer in his own bailiwick represents the country much like an ambassador. Within reason, therefore, he should be allotted enough money to enable him to keep up with the influential in his community as far as the quality of his housing and entertainment are concerned. You can't win friends and influence foreigners serving hamburgers and coke.

In this regard the Bahamians are no different than anyone else, but that's where the similarity ends. In the Bahamas you can ask for something in a store, and they will tell you they don't carry it anymore because they never could

As bringer of the Word

keep it in stock. They speak a wonderful, lilting English, but their own brand—words such as "swift" for quick, "reach" for arrive, and "mash" for runover. There are many more, some quite unexpected. We once chartered a boat that the captain, at full speed, piled up on a rock off Rose Island, near Nassau. As the boat began to sink, the captain reassured us that there was "no cause to be frustrated!" Two local maxims involving goats give the flavor of the islands. "Loose goat never know how tie goat feel" and "Good nature give Nanny goat short tail." Both are worthy of Pascal's *Pensées*.

United States defense interests in the Bahamas were increasing at the time of my arrival. Chief among these was the project known as AUTEC, the Atlantic Underwater Test and Evaluation Center, a joint American-British Navy program having as its base the "tongue of the ocean" —a mile deep ocean trench two miles wide between the islands of New Providence and Andros.

AUTEC was really big time. If the defense of the western world depends in large part on its missile-firing nuclear submarines, these must be able to travel about undetected. In my day in Nassau our first-line-of-defense submarines rattled through the water like old washing machines, and the presumption was that sophisticated Soviet listening devices could spot them like so many sitting ducks. In order to reduce their noise, the Navy needed a large natural "bathtub" in which to do its testing. The "tongue of the ocean" was just that. An alternative site was off the Aleutian Islands and another was in the Puerto Rican trough, but British Navy interest and the physical features of the "tongue"—the sides of the "bathtub" go straight down close to the Andros shore—made the Bahamas first choice.

There was only one problem—and this is where I got into the act—the Bay Street Boys didn't want any part of

AUTEC. They were all making a killing out of tourism and were fearful that anything to do with submarines in the middle of their tourist paradise would frighten off the golden trade. In our negotiations for the site, we had the anomaly of the British delegation (made up of Royal Navy representatives and Bahamians) sitting across the table from the United States, whereas it should have been ourselves and the Royal Navy on one side and the Bahamians on the other. After considerable perfidy on all sides, the deal finally went through. (The British didn't exactly give us the site, although their Navy benefited totally from our expertise. We understated to the Bahamians what would be going on, and the Bahamians dragged their feet trying to get the most out of it that they could.)

If by now our submarines slip silently in and out of Kronstadt Harbor, the Navy technicians are the obvious heroes. My own minor role, however, was cited in a Post Inspection Report which stated that "successful negotiation of the AUTEC agreement was due in considerable part to the Principal Officer's understanding of the factors involved and his close relationship with Bahamian personalities." I mention these kind words not to blow my own horn (although it is a little toot) but primarily to put them on record in view of some shoddy treatment I received later at the hands of the Department.

While all this sinister underwater activity was taking place, life on the surface in Nassau continued in a round of gaiety. Technically speaking, Government House stood at the apex of the social life of Nassau. When the Duke of Windsor was the incumbent Governor, this was undoubtedly true in actual fact. By the time we reached Nassau, however, the incumbents were all honest but humble knights and, although they were the Queen's own representatives, the apex had moved elsewhere—notably just across the street.

Dorothy Killam, reputed by some to be the richest woman in the world, was certainly one of Nassau's great hostesses. Dorothy's deceased husband was Canadian and, like so many Canadians, owned most of Canada, which gave her scope. Her dinners were usually for thirty to forty people who were seated at two enormous round tables in the garden. The tables were so big that a servant had to walk out over the tablecloth to fix the flowers in the center-piece. The servant wore special white cotton socks for this operation. It was a nice touch. The house was an old Bahamian type with a verandah and stairs leading down to the garden. Centered in the patio and separating the two tables was a large circular bed of yuccas, each spike of which was adorned with a freshly picked hibiscus flower. The effect, as one descended the staircase, was lavish in the extreme—the hibiscus lit from above, the silver place settings gleaming in the candlelight, and at least half a dozen white-coated waiters standing behind each table.

Protocol, of course, looms large at this kind of entertainment. My first night at Mrs. Killam's, Eric Dudley (the Earl of) was the guest of honor. He leaned over after the ladies had left and said, "Hrumph, I'm glad to see an English Earl still takes precedence over an American Vice-Consul." In vain I pointed out to him that there had been a mistake with my card, implying that things would have been very different had it been made out correctly. He looked at me with a wondering, fishy stare, as if I must be joking. Earls are like that—they can only be quelled by a duke or a marquis.

We had a belt of earls one night at home—three of them (Nassau used to abound in them). To my surprise, the three were meek as lambs when confronted by a formidable grande dame from New York, one with both presence and bulk. I really felt quite proud of her until she got out of hand later in the evening. After dinner one of the guests, a talented but temperamental Hungarian painter who had brought along his violin, played the last movement from Brahms' Concerto in D—a piece that requires an accomplished virtuoso rendition. After he gave his all in a whirlwind finish worthy of Carnegie Hall and then took a deep bow, the distinguished old trout from New York, who had been dozing throughout his performance, opened her eyes and in a voice accustomed to command said: "Young man, would you play 'La Vie en Rose'." It's things like this that give us a bad name with Europeans. The Hungarian marched out of the room in high dudgeon at having been taken for a paid hand and only returned after a sulky walk in the garden because he wanted to sell us a picture.

One night at the golf club in Lyford Cay I sat next to the Duchess of Windsor under very false pretenses. The dinner was given by Eric Dudley (the earl with the fishy stare) who was an old friend of the Windsors. Unfortunately, Eric had been taken ill that afternoon and, as some kind of a compromise candidate, I had been catapulted up from the ranks to take his place at the table. The Duchess of Windsor, rather small but very chic, looked at my card as I sat down in the host's chair. "Bernard?" she said with a questioning inflexion and the accent on the second syllable, which I consider wrong. "No, Ma'am," I said, giving her the royal treatment, "*Bar*nard, like the college in New York." She batted her eyes and smiled coquettishly. "Oh," she said, then quick as a flash, "mine's Windsor, like the Castle." She is a woman of great charm, and we got on famously after this little interchange. When the soup came, however, the man on her right, who was trying to make Admiral on his first cruise, monopolized her for the rest of the evening. It was probably all to the good that I never talked to the Duchess again as I was about to suggest a project that might not have gone down too well. What I had in mind was the manufacture of little stuffed replicas of the

Duke, complete with changes of clothing, and their sale for the charity of her choice. Never have I seen a more perfectly attired, neater little man, with beautiful tiny shoes. It might have been an expensive package, but they would have gone like hot cakes.

Gambling in the Bahamas took on a more sinister aspect at a Vegas-like casino in Freeport toward the end of our second year. Before then gambling had been restricted to the old Bahamian Club in Nassau, a peerless night spot just out of town on West Bay Street. The club purveyed the best of food and drink and Meyer Davis-type music, a black tie was required for dinner and dancing (one gentleman always wore tails) and the slot machines were kept to a minimum. The manager-owner, a Scot named MacKenzie from Providence, Rhode Island, used to plead with the customers not to gamble—"Don't do it," he'd say. "You can't possibly win." It was a marvelous place to go after an evening elsewhere. Unfortunately, a few years later Mac was made an offer he couldn't refuse and, shortly thereafter, the old club was razed. It was superseded by an enormous establishment on Paradise Island, very inconvenient for dropping in, if you lived in Nassau. Rumors were rife that the Mafia had moved into the Freeport casinos and were using the profits to further their criminal activities in the States. The head man was reported to be Meyer Lansky in Florida, whose coffers were replenished weekly by a courier carrying the loot.

Official British attitude toward all this was remarkably insular. In the first place, the Governor flatly refused to believe that Meyer Lansky existed. Furthermore, the Governor's idea of crooked gambling was a croupier palming a card or pressing a lever to control the ball in roulette. As long as the customer was protected from this kind of hanky-panky, he felt the operation was clean. He had assigned two ex-policemen from Singapore to the casinos to insure there was always fair play. Jolly drinking companions, neither of them in my opinion were up to the higher flights of chicanery as represented by the "skim." Technically, a "skim" is the unaccounted removal of a percentage of the day's take after the casino is closed down. Presumably, it takes place in the inner recesses of the counting house and nobody knows about it at all—least of all the two gentlemen from Singapore. I wrote a report on the situation entitled "Bahamas Green Felt Jungle." I thought it would cause a sensation in Washington, but nobody paid any attention. It wasn't until years later that poor old Meyer Lansky had trouble finding a homeland.

I once had drinks with some mobsters who were leaving the Islands, having lost out in their bid for control. This group lived briefly in a sumptuous beach cottage built by friends of ours who enjoyed it one year before getting divorced. The new tenants transformed its former romantic aura with so many searchlights that the house stood in a pool of light making it impossible for anyone to approach undetected. Although their armpits bulged suspiciously and their presumed wives were obviously call girls from Miami, the "boys" seemed a simple, straightforward lot. In the course of one conversation with a burly, square-faced henchman, the subject of impartial British justice in the Bahamas came up as a topic. The henchman dismissed it airily—"You know who killed your father or your brother. Who needs impartial justice?"

Nassau, however, was a hotbed of far more devious types than these blunt soldiers of fortune. At that time financial shenanigans on the grand scale were made possible by a certain legal leniency on the part of government. It always seemed to me that a child of two who sold tootsie rolls could incorporate in the Bahamas. Operating through banks and trust companies with the most reputable sounding names, the devious ones never seemed to transgress any laws, although most of them were wanted in their countries of origin. One efficient combination consisted of two partners, one of whom could never set foot in the United States and the other was barred from Canada. The Canadian exile handled the United States side of the business and his partner went in and out of Canada at will. Needless to say they flourished.

Paradise Island, that undistinguished bit of real estate now connected by a bridge to New Providence, was formerly known as Hog Island until transformed by my old school chum, Huntington Hartford. Probably the best item in the Hartford complex was then the Café Martinique. Situated on a lagoon dug by Axel Wennergren (there was a popular fantasy that he had constructed it to hide U-boats in World War II), the Martinique had a delightful red plush decor with deep black leather armchairs in the bar and a gaslight ambiance making one feel in the heart of Victorian France. Music was supplied by a group of Hungarian gypsies. The first night there I tipped the zither player rather lavishly with the result that, whenever I appeared in the place afterwards, he would strike up my favorite number. My Martinique equivalent of "Hail to the Chief" when translated meant "At the gate," but one shouldn't be thrown off by this prosaic nomenclature. It is the epitome of the wild and longing.

A peak night at the Martinique came with the filming of *Thunderball*, the James Bond spectacular. For extras in a nightclub scene at the Martinique, about two hundred smartly dressed ladies and gentlemen, of different age groups, were delivered lock, stock and barrel by the local Red Cross from among its supporters, in return for a flat donation by the producers of one thousand pounds if the cargo arrived intact. The script called for Bond and his girl friend to arrive by speedboat in the lagoon in front of the club. But movie-making is a tedious business and their arrival was held up endlessly by some technical hitch. Box suppers were provided for the extras, but their cheer was minimal. As the hours wore on while we waited for Bond to appear, the bar flourished. An old friend, Sir John Carden, and I had been whiling away the time playing backgammon, but John had also been applying himself to the bottle, which made him somewhat restive. Always a nervous man, the enforced wait had gotten to him and, in the course of our gaming, he attempted several times to call a "water taxi" to get him back to New Providence (the bridge was not yet built). Water taxis may exist in Venice and the posher parts of Florida, but they are nonexistent in Nassau. I thought it best to humor him, however, as we had been hanging around since 7:00 P.M. It must have been close to 2:00 A.M. when John suddenly pushed back the table, tottered to his feet, and announced—"I simply can't stand it another minute." Out he stalked like Ichabod Crane and down the steps into the full glare of klieg lights and cameras grinding. Bond's speedboat, at long last, was just approaching the dock. John, waving his arm wildly, of course assumed that his water taxi had finally materialized.

"Taxi! Taxi!" shouted Sir John.

"Cut!" cried Terrence Young, the director. Everything ground to a halt. "Who the hell is that idiot?"

"I am Sir John Carden," replied John with considerable hauteur. But it was an unusual dialogue, however, as Young had the microphone.

"Take him out to sea and dump him," said Young.

One hour and thousands of dollars later they ran through it again, but John was fast asleep. An assistant director in a small boat had run him back to Nassau. Arrogance in the raw can sometimes be delightful.

My only other experience with the movies took place on a West Bay Street traffic circle where Kennedy, Macmillan and Diefenbaker (Canada) planted three ornamental trees to commemorate their Nassau meeting. I had to make a little speech of acceptance for the trees and accompanying plaque. I've never been much of an orator—my children curl up on the floor in horror whenever I've had to make a public utterance. It came as a bit of surprise to me, therefore, that while I was mouthing a few platitudes, I noticed that the few people who had gathered together for our little ceremony were being steadily augmented by others on bicycles and by groups getting out of their cars. By the time I had finished, the audience must have at least tripled. To say I was touched might be going too far, but I did feel my charisma had come a long way since my Sixth Form speech at school. After shaking hands with various Rotarian dignitaries, I noticed that the crowd had suddenly evaporated. Crowds generally disperse in all directions, but this one was moving off in a block. Apparently they had thought we were the Beatles. The latter, I was told, were filming *Help!* a little farther up the road.

Most people are destined to live on the periphery of world events. I found this particularly true with regard to the Cuban missile crisis. Just below Nassau in the waters surrounding Cuba, the United States had deployed twenty-five destroyers, two cruisers, several submarines, at least two carriers, and a fleet of support ships. If the Russians insisted on breaking through this barrier with their missile cargo it looked as if the balloon would go up. Pondering the question one silent moonlit night, I was joined on the verandah at home by our dog, Buster, who was half-boxer and half-African ridgeback. We both enjoyed these late-night sessions contemplating the infinite. Sitting beside me, his noble, flattopped head held in heraldic pose made a perfect end table for a drink. I think he liked the coolness just above his furrowed brow. I was reminded of that time on the houseboat in Kashmir when the major-

Swimming with Buster

domo and I talked about Nirvana. If the Russians ran our Cuban blockade, this could be Armageddon. Out of the piled up dead, I thought of the souls released. Could this be a viable concept? I looked at Buster with my glass on his head. He had a worried expression. I turned to the practicalities.

If the balloon went up, Nassau, which imports almost all its food, would be starving in no time at all. We had Emergency Evacuation plans in the office for all American citizens. This involved the commercial airlines and the Navy, but in a sudden nuclear holocaust, Nassau might well be forgotten. Besides, in an exchange of missiles, no Russian and/or Cuban would waste one on the Bahamas. Miami and the Eastern seaboard were much more likely targets. If the worst came to the worst we might be better off here. Food was the chief problem. I decided to buy a fishing rod to supplement what would be a skimpy diet. Just off the house in the waters inside the reef were a clump of rocks that harbored a school of angelfish and sometimes a wandering grouper. (These clumps of rock used to be called "nigger heads." "Coral heads" is the present terminology, as "black heads" would never do.) The next day, not being much of a fisherman, I was easy prey for the salesman in the local hardware store who outfitted me with a collapsible rod and spinning reel, all neatly packaged and to my mind just the thing for survival. On getting home that evening, I opened the package and had a trial run assembling the contraption. I should note here that mechanical ability is not my forte. I could easily fit together the three pieces of rod, but attaching the reel to the rod was quite another matter. Whatever I did, the thing seemed to be upside down. I finally gave it up in disgust. After several more unsuccessful attempts on successive days, it was with great relief that I learned that the missile crisis had passed. If push had come to shove, I sometimes wonder whether my plan would have been feasible. In the back of my mind I have the impression that angelfish are inedible. People fret about the periphery, but sometimes it's not a bad place to be.

Oddly enough, in the course of my brief diplomatic career, I only served in countries under a monarchical form of government, a rarity these days—Belgium, The Netherlands Antilles, and the Crown Colony of the Bahamas. To be sure, the last two are considerably removed from their respective thrones, but in the final analysis the allegiance of each is to their Queen. My acquaintance with any of the ruling houses in question was peripheral indeed; I was scarcely the confidant of kings. Once in Antwerp on the Scheldt river I was on a boat with the King of the Belgians and a few hundred others looking at some lock that was being opened. The King and I exchanged no words at all. We must have shaken hands. In Aruba, I jollied it up with Prince Bernhard of the Netherlands along the following lines:

JLB (thinking of my Dutch friend Jan vander Mortel who had been something at the court in his youth): "How is our mutual friend, Jan?"

Prince Bernhard (blankly): "Jan? Jan who? My dear fellow, I must know three thousand Jans."

Prince Philip and I did better, or rather Diana did. We were having dinner on board the royal yacht *Britannia* in Nassau harbor and were standing in the main salon awaiting Philip's arrival. Everyone was dressed to the nines— white tie and decorations for the men, long white gloves for the ladies. My decorations consisted of a discreet row of miniatures, one medal for joining the army, one for defending the United States, one for winning the war, and one for having a good secretary. Everybody in the armed forces was entitled to the first three, still they added a bit of color. (It's surprising how many major generals use these footling items to swell their many-tiered rows.) Medals that are round mean nothing; they have to be crosses or stars. Philip, of course, would know this, but then I wasn't posing as a warrior.

Diana and I as a couple must have looked more viable, conversationally, than the other guests because Philip, after shaking hands all around, came back to us and we chatted about his recent trip to Canada where there had been some unpleasantness in Quebec with French secessionists.

"It must be terrible," said Diana, "going somewhere and knowing you may be shot or bombed."

"Oh it's not so bad," said Philip. "After all there are certain ancillary benefits." He smiled.

I followed his gaze into the dining salon where the yacht's orchestra was playing and, behind each seat, at attention, was a red-coated aide or equerry bedizened with medals—all of them crosses or stars. It's nice to see a prince enjoying the perquisites of office.

The assassination of President Kennedy sent a shudder through Nassau along with the rest of the world. Diana and I were having lunch at home prior to attending the Bahamian Police games, when Alfred, the butler, told us in a voice so hushed he could hardly be heard. The news had just come over the kitchen radio. Almost immediately the phone began ringing and continued to ring all afternoon. The curious thing was that practically everyone who called seemed to come from the borderline disturbed element, of which Nassau had quite a few. The shooting apparently tipped their finely balanced scales and reduced them to near hysteria. I prepared a statement for ZNS, the local radio station. This was no longer periphery, this was real. I had to say something. At five o'clock that evening, after a brief introduction by the Governor, I read off the following:

"The tragic death of President Kennedy today has

shocked the world. On behalf of all Americans I would like to thank those who have expressed their sympathy in our moment of loss. Regardless of their political belief, all Americans are united in grief over this desperate act.

"With the playing of the 'Star-Spangled Banner,' after the announcement of the President's death, there comes a feeling to each of us—what now?

"I would like to quote from Mr. Kennedy's Thanksgiving proclamation the following: 'Yet, as our power has grown, so has our peril.'

"That has been proved today. The President has paid the price for what he goes on to give thanks for in his message, namely 'the decency of purpose, steadfastness of resolve and strength of will which the American people have inherited.'

"I will conclude by saying, though we have lost a great leader, we will close ranks behind this ideal. Our prayers go out now for the thirty-sixth President of the United States, Lyndon B. Johnson."

I could say that I resigned from the State Department because of the dissolution of Camelot, but my reasons for doing so were somewhat more personal. The phone rang one day and a voice told me that I was being recalled to Washington to head up something called the Correspondence Branch. Apparently a computer had gone into action and my name came up as having been a writer—just what you need for correspondence. The voice told me it was important work answering letters from people who objected to the Administration's position on Vietnam. As I didn't think much of our Vietnam policy either, this little aside gave me pause. Also conditioning my reaction was the fact that a Foreign Service Officer is not without honor, save in his own country. Abroad, the FSO lives well, at home I wouldn't even get a parking space. These, however, were minor considerations.

While waiting for my name to appear on the next promotion list, I received a letter from Personnel saying that I had been rated by the Promotion Board in the bottom tenth of my class. Now I'm a most retiring man, but this seemed to be going too far, particularly since the post had been given an excellent report by a team of Foreign Service Inspectors. These Inspectors are knowledgeable, senior FSOs who spend at least a week at each post looking into everything from one's wife's chitchat to where the Martindale-Hubbell is kept. (The latter is a list of American lawyers and is about as useful as an old Sears Roebuck catalogue.) In my reply to Personnel, I quoted liberally from the Inspection Report—"Leadership is imaginative, politically intuitive and relaxed . . . discipline and morale are superlative . . . political and economic reporting is some of the best seen during his inspection year." (Toot! Toot! Toot!) Shortly thereafter an apologetic reply came back from Washington stating that a thorough investigation revealed that the Board had gotten me mixed up with another. Apparently this "other" was some character considered weak on judgement—at one post he predicted a revolution that never materialized and at another he tried to seduce the Ambassador's wife. Washington "sincerely regretted the anguish this unfortunate occurrence had caused me." The anguish was minimal, but the loss of faith was extreme.

Once you lose faith in the management of anything, it's best to clear out, take stock, review the bidding, etc. Besides, if I didn't really have to, why spend my declining years in some such place as Aden, where I was sure I would be sent if I rejected their offer. Why not retire to my "estates"? The phrase had a nice ring to it, connoting Marlborough and Blenheim. I had been out of the country ten

years, and though it might be stretching things a bit, I had done the state some service. Furthermore, I was no captain of industry who would go crazy doing nothing. The change would be imperceptible. The outward and visible signs of accomplishment had never been my strong point. My enjoyment was me. I was the constant in the equations.

It came as a shock, I confess, to realize the passage of time. In terms of Shakespeare's ages of man I was about to enter the sixth—and next to last! The "lean and slippered pantaloon" might still be a distant cloud, but the thought of this jumpsuit for our golden years gave me a tiny *frisson*.

CHAPTER

10

When you retire, unless you can manage it early enough, there's an uncomfortable feeling that you are reaching the end of the road and that the grim reaper is just around the corner. To combat this, you have to assume a role. You can become a hopeless drunk or chase little girls. Neither can be fully endorsed since the potential for trouble is enormous. You may turn into an indefatigable golfer, gardener, sailor, or horseman, but the dogged pursuit of excellence in any one line can be a tiresome hangup. It is better by far to be the poor man's "Renaissance Man," ineptly doing them all. Too many with minimal ability make themselves miserable striving to excel. I suggest, therefore, the role of country squire.

Practically anyone can be a passable country squire. You don't even have to live in the country. A semblance of country helps, but all you really need is an old coat, maybe a pipe, possibly a dog. It's all in your approach. I have a privet bush at home, trimmed in the shape of an obelisk, that makes me think of the Sitwells' "Renishaw" in England. All the piled-up magnificence of this great country seat, the sweep of land and possessions, can be caught in a bit of privet if you can but focus your perspectives. I've had long training in this type of legerdemain, starting with "fishing through the ice" in Central Park.

Ideally, a proper country squire should have roots where he is living. In this aspect I am somewhat hampered because the ancestral home of my family, a seventeenth-century landmark in Hartford, Connecticut, was torn down in 1898 to make way for a hospital. This was the house bought by Captain John Barnard at the time of the French and Indian Wars. Had the house been extant, I would probably not have been happy in it. Photographs taken prior to demolition reveal some handsome paneling, but the ceilings were so low that the rooms look as though they should have been inhabited by Beatrix Potter mice. The only place a tall man could have stood was inside the fireplace. Since I had never been to Hartford in my life and prefer to be near the sea, I felt no compulsion to resuscitate these roots. Some ten years ago, while still in the service, I bought a substitute ancestral home outside of Stonington, Connecticut. Although it was built much later than the house in Hartford, it has long tall windows down to the floor, and the sea is two minutes away.

I think my forebear, the armigerous Richard, would approve of "Red Brook" (our place in Stonington). Situated on a slight rise above the road, the house is indubitably a "manor"—a two-storied square block with a cupola and four chimneys rising out of the balustraded roof. Below, on the front facade, Ionic pillars support a shallow balcony, also balustraded, over the door. In short, it is pure Greek Revival—that architectural reflection in wood that developed in America and Russia early in the nineteenth century as part of the general enthusiasm for classical antiquity.

Beyond the house, the land dips away into what I fondly think of as the park. Actually, the area is a swamp with a brook running through it that was once the scene of an Indian massacre which gave the place its name. (It's not clear whether Indians massacred settlers, or vice versa, just that the brook ran red.) The land rises on the farther side

"Red Brook"

in a shallow, bowl-like contour, with open fields in the middle and a wood on either side. Within the bowl are a farmhouse and a renovated barn, both of which are occupied in the summer by two of my daughters and their husbands, who come up weekends from the city; it's a family compound.

Nearby is the village of Stonington, known as the "Borough," a former New England fishing village that hit it big in the days of whaling. Too far away from both Boston and New York to be a bedroom for either, much of its original seafaring charm remains. During the day, when the wind is in the wrong direction, you can hear unfortunately the steady drone of traffic on U.S. 1, but at night Stonington noises come into their own—the deep, sonorous foghorn on Watch Hill, the hoot of the lesser horn on the outer breakwater, and the idle clang of the bell buoy marking the harbor entrance. The night freights moan their whistles at the railroad crossings, on either side of town, and long after the train has passed, you can still hear the rumble of car wheels receding in the distance. Day breaks with the yacketing of gulls and then the mourning doves.

Tony Bailey has written the definitive work on Stonington, excerpts from which appeared in *The New Yorker*. I will only add a footnote here in the form of a personal note that I received years ago from an unknown visionary in Ohio who wanted to promote "a small antique styled town just a quarter of a mile off main highway. To consist of several small well-built dwellings, one fine Tea Room Tavern, and one enterprize corporation to make a useful article. Would like to have it occupied by some book writers, artists, some plain good people, and some tall athletic people. Enclosed please find 10¢ for postage and trouble."

Although the "Borough" might be a little weak on "plain good people," this sums up Stonington pretty well. The American Velvet Company, our one local industry, presumably produces a useful article—they use a lot of it in caskets.

Menacing the area at large is the Eastern seaboard's creeping megalopolis, which will triumph in the end, but one can still find outside the "Borough" the illusion of country living. One ten-acre field next to our house has two cows on it that give a pleasing rural effect. I have the loan of the cows from a professional farmer a mile up the road in return for the hay from my field, which he cuts and stores for himself. This arrangement is obviously all to the good for him. On my side of the ledger, I manage to achieve my rural effect at a minimal expense. I don't have to pay someone to cut the field, the cows keep it down and fertilize it. There are no labor costs because—and this is the important gimmick—the cows are pregnant and don't need to be milked. The farmer knows to the minute when they are going to drop a calf and arrives with a substitute cow. He removes the animals when the weather becomes inclement. No need for barns, feed, and so forth. When I talk to other cattlemen, I know of none with fewer troubles.

Someone once said we must incorporate our illusions and look beyond them. The trouble is, looking beyond this particular illusion, I can envision the same field at some future date with twenty A-frame houses. Nevertheless, as of now, "Red Brook" provides me with what every man needs at times, namely "a quiet citadel in which to stand aloof."

My friend and neighbor, Rust Hills, who has written a fine book on retiring, takes as his guru, Montaigne. I rather favor Lucretius. He goes on with his citadel concept—"stoutly fortified by the teachings of the wise, one gazes down from that elevation on others wandering aimlessly . . . pitting their wits one against another, disputing for precedence, struggling night and day with unstinted effort to scale the pinnacles of wealth and power." A fearsome picture! And true enough today to turn any youth into a hopeless junkie unless he's a keen competitor. Some people thrive on competition, but I think it may well be what's wrong with the country. Horace Walpole puts it nicely: "Ambition blushes, but I never had any . . . I was born at the top of the world. I have long been nobody and am charmed to be so."

Standing aloof in my citadel, as Lucretius recommends, I ask myself what, if anything, has been learned from this meander through life. Not much. I know, of course, that man cannot live by hors d'oeuvres alone—and all that kind of thing. After all, I went to a church school. Certain big, glarmy subjects loom, however, such as the topics one gravitates towards late at night—sex, love, death, God, the infinite—not to mention politics, war and the state of the nation. The best way of handling them is to keep them down in your subconscious and concentrate on the batting averages. Be that as it may, "fortified by the teachings of the wise," herewith my own approach to some of these hardy perennials.

In any intimate man-woman relationship, there are three circles of endeavor—sex, love, and for those over thirty, marriage. Marriage makes the subject more complicated because it involves criteria extraneous to the first two— money, status, security, friends, etc. The trick, or ideal, is to intertwine the three circles. The Germans, who love anything to do with the psyche, may have a word for it— *gemütlichpretzelmachen.*

First, let us consider sex. It has been my experience that men are the victims of women in matters sexual. Somewhere, probably in the French salons, women put across the idea that every woman is basically sexy, that each is some sort of Stradivarius, requiring only a master to play her. I consider this to be totally false. There is great variation in the sexiness of women. I remember a *poule* in Paris, a round, chunky little girl with a pink ribbon at the back of her head and a ponytail that came to her waist. She insisted, of course, on my buying some terrible champagne, but we got on rather well. A jolly girl who enjoyed her work, she was inordinately proud of her *"bouton électrique,"* which was indeed large. One of a family of nine children who were brought up on a farm outside of Lyons, she preferred her present life. She told me with a note of pride that we were in the best house in Paris, that they were very good to her, and that she had met a lot of interesting people. I asked her if she minded going to bed with different men each night. She looked at me quizzically. "Mind?" she said, and burst out laughing. "I love it! All the time one person? Bah! I was married once. *J'en ai eu jusqu'aux dents!"*

Some women's lives revolve around sex, they think of nothing else. Others never think of it at all. Of the two types, one is obviously better off with the former, providing the lady is sufficiently fastidious to concentrate her favors on oneself alone. Given the basic premise, it may be solace on a doubtful bosom, but as long as the attraction lasts those whom sex has joined together, no man can put asunder. I understand that certain aboriginal tribes base their marriage rituals on a belief in its permanence.

I've forgotten what Tin Pan Alley decided about love (Mencken dismissed it as perceptual anaesthesia), but Ernest Becker's phrase "a cosmology of two" seems to me the best description. La Rochefoucauld considers it impermanent, but an almost tangible phenomenon: "In their first passion women love their lovers, in the others they love love." Louise Brogan in one of her poems says: "Love comes in at the eyes and subdues the body." Anna Karenina loved Vronsky "as only a woman can for whom love outweighs every other good thing in life." Is all this more than having the "hots" for another? It's debatable. The down-to-earth would define love as being turned on by someone companionable. Certainly a delight in holding hands and dreaming of the other when apart stem from these two ingredients. Possibly, only one is necessary. Tristan and Isolde are not renowned for their wide range of interests. On the other hand, the romantic believe that love adds a new dimension. Being in love is elation on seeing the loved one, it's not caring where you are as long as you are together. In short, it is probably a disease—sometimes incurable, but seldom fatal.

Years ago on the boat coming back from Japan, that girl with the jade pendant said she couldn't figure out whether she loved me because of our wonderful sexual relationship or whether that was wonderful because she loved me. The remark underscores the problem. Both urges are inextricably entwined, and you can't really enjoy one without the other. The love object must be held, and sex needs that something in the eyes that makes the holding count.

Love, of course, is a tiny, overburdened word. You can love the Redskins, Berlioz, your children. You can even have love as an ethic. You love your partner in life. As a matter of fact, my wife and I are so much the same person that there is no distinction between us, except on superficials like strength of character, honesty and concern. She is also pleasing to the eye, and, if I do say so, distinguée. All my encompassing love of self takes in this other self. We have shared our world a long time. We look out on it as a unit. Frank Crowninshield said that married men make very poor husbands, and I have not been the best. According to Bertrand Russell, sincere affection for one person does not preclude attraction to another. Nevertheless inside my citadel I have an inner keep, where there happens just to be two there.

In close proximity to this inner keep are the children and, although from time to time we view one another clinically, we are bound together by empathy. We know and enjoy each other's foibles. I've found, however, that in a tight-knit family group there is nothing like a foible or two to destroy one's father image. Our youngest daughter evidently thought the same because she invented out of whole cloth a fantasy father, a hero of the Bataan death march, and told her husband never to mention it as presumably the memories would upset me! Our eldest always used to dream of a *Saturday Evening Post* cover showing a father and mother benignly smiling as they enter the dining room with the Thanksgiving turkey.

The nearest we came to this tableau was several years ago when we tried a suckling pig for Christmas. I was about to say my daughter Sylvia prepared it during her brief cooking phase. (She is one of those with intense, short-lived interests. The only reminder of her absorption in cooking is a six-tiered rack of spices and an array of copper pots, some of them never used.) But actually her husband and Diana cooked it, staying up until 2:00 A.M. Regrettably, before serving the next day, they decided to carve it in the kitchen, whereupon the pig literally disintegrated. Its head fell over on the side of the plate and the apple, no longer in its mouth, looked like a stray bit of garbage. Temperament runs high in the holiday season, and as a family unit we almost flew apart when my mother-in-law gently asked whether it had been run over by a truck.

To celebrate that Yuletide season, one evening after dinner we smoked pot *en famille*. Given the tempers roused by the fate of the pig, I felt that this mass indulgence in narcotics could be an error, but the spirit of scientific inquiry prevailed and we settled down cozily about the fire in the library. All very Dickensian. As the fire crackled merrily, my youngest son-in-law produced a packet of Acapulco Gold that his sister had given him for Christmas. None of us had had pot before, so our curiosity was mixed with some apprehension. I first thought one of my old pipes

would be the best method of indoctrination—shades of
kicking the gong around—but after diligently puffing away
for a good five minutes, the residue in the pipe took over
and the flame went out. Nothing had happened at all. We
next tried making a "joint" by opening up a Camel cigarette and pasting the paper around the marijuana with
rubber cement. Again much puffing and inhaling by all
concerned. Diana had a cold and refrained from smoking,
as did our youngest daughter, Pamela, who was pregnant.
Her decision seemed sensible at the time and we all agreed,
although on what medical basis it is difficult to say. I suppose ten minutes must have gone by and I was in the process of pronouncing the experiment a washout when suddenly I burst into giggles. The producer of the pot was a
giggler, too. No sooner had I been seized than he doubled
up laughing himself, so much so that he had to retire to the
hall where he presumably rocked back and forth in splendid isolation. My giggles subsided as suddenly as they had
come. My other son-in-law and Sylvia had an entirely different reaction. My daughter sank lower and lower in her
chair and announced that the corner of the room up near
the ceiling was expanding and contracting. Her husband
said he saw it, too, and started taking notes on a yellow
pad. It made him feel sexy, he said. At this point the
giggler returned from the hall looking quite composed, but
immediately broke up again. This set me off in a renewed
spasm. Meanwhile Sylvia sat staring owl-like at the wall,
while her mate fidgeted and scribbled away at his notes.
These turned out to be gibberish, which was odd, as he is a
most articulate man. Then it passed—no more wave-like
occurrences—and the males retired to the cellar to play
bumper pool. The gigglers consumed a can of peanuts,
avidly, and were roundly defeated by the non-giggler. The
latter not only wanted no peanuts, but said he saw blue
darts of flame off the end of his cue showing him the proper

angle to hit the ball. The whole episode could not have taken more than three-quarters of an hour. There were no aftereffects, nor did I have any desire to have another. Marijuana could be beneficial for drunks to keep them off the booze, but in my estimation, for sociable enjoyment, it will never take the place of a dry martini on the rocks.

I feel quite strongly about the latter. In this day and age when so much is crashing around us, we should be eternally grateful to the genius who first poured his martini into an old-fashioned glass filled with ice. Looking back on the days when we used to drink them straight up, it makes me shudder to think of the increased mayhem that would have occurred had not this unknown man revolutionized our habits several decades ago. There are three modern benefactors of mankind who have greatly improved the quality of life for many. I would put him foremost among them. In my triptych he would get the center panel, flanked by two lesser figures—the inventors of the golf cart and the roller furling jib. Purists, I know, will scoff at these last two as being exemplars of the general decadence, but if we take into consideration the number of aging sportsmen, who would be sailing boring catboats or not playing golf at all without these innovations, I think on balance their inventors also deserve some form of canonization.

"The world," said Walpole, "is a comedy to those that think, a tragedy to those that feel." Some people do go in heavily for feeling. They have an inclination towards the dark and revel in it. Feeling, to be sure, is the essence of our being, our sexuality, our creative urge in all directions —we can't do without it, but I agree with Walpole. People who feel deeply generally take themselves too seriously, and if you do that, you're headed for tragedy. Think of poor Dylan Thomas, a feeler if there ever was one, raging against the dying of the light.

The deep feelers also are a menace to others and get us

into a lot of trouble. Eric Hoffer comments that we live in an "apocalyptic madhouse staged by maniacal saviors of humanity." Quite a mouthful, but true. The only refuge, he says, is "absorption in the minutiae of existence." Although Hoffer uses the phrase to connote a dismal last ditch stand, I think we've got something here, something I've been saying all along: in the minutiae we find enjoyment. As David Reisman says, we need "a happier sense of the ordinary."

"What joy it is," Lucretius writes, "when the storm-winds are lashing the waters, to gaze from the shore at the heavy stress some other man is enduring!" He's not being unpleasant, he is just glad not to be there himself. Sometimes in the morning I turn over in bed and switch on the radio for the helicopter report on traffic conditions. To snuggle down and press one's cheek in the pillow while a truck is stalled in the right-hand lane of the Major Deegan Expressway can be joy indeed.

Granted, you need to be retired or out of work or just plain shiftless to indulge in the above exercise, but the need for some such approach is essential. Ever since the great depression, enormous strides have been taken to alleviate the lot of the poor. The people I worry about are those who know where their next meal is coming from. People who really need money always have a goal in life—more money—and therefore, unless hopelessly downtrodden, lead reasonably happy, purposeful lives in its pursuit. The well-off, by contrast, are frequently most unhappy. Some take to drink, others drugs, some work themselves to death (workaholics), many are divorced at least once and the suicide rate of this class is rising. "When God went off in despair, Crow stropped his beak and started in on the two thieves." Thus saith Ted Hughes in *Crow*.

This widespread malaise is nothing new. In Dr. Johnson's day they used to call it melancholy. People were constantly being seized with fits of melancholy. In Johnson's case Boswell diagnosed it as a horror of life in general— again all those jagged rocks beneath the surface of the ice. I was once in a hospital where they wheeled out an old man to air in the hall each day as they made up his room. Slumped in his wheelchair with eyes half-shut, he would drone in monotone day after day, "Oh God, let me die. Oh God, please let me die . . ." The repetition was searing. What was his pain and loss in life? What were they doing to him? There is plenty of Johnson's horror around, but we can't let it get us down. Suffice it to say, the old man was not a cheery note in the corridor.

For most of us who, in one way or another, have tuned our lives to gratification here (and we are a goodly number), death does not come as a release. Although maybe there is a "beyond," it's more likely that the unfortunate invented the concept, hoping for something better. In order to prove the "hereafter," some will point to our ability to distinguish right from wrong. This attribute, they say, must have come from God, the inference being there is some cozy corner up there where God metes out rewards and punishments. People say they couldn't live with themselves if they did such and such, but there is nothing spiritual here. I could always live with myself no matter what I did. My inner friend and I could invent all kinds of excuses. This is not to say we have no sense of ethics. We do. Things like lying, cheating, cruelty, and killing are bad. What is good is another matter. Maybe just the absence of bad. Unfortunately, ethics, or more properly metaethics, seems to me a word game invented by the Greeks who have always liked to sit around and talk. Deceit is the kinder side of infidelity . . . you can go right down the list of the bad, showing how each could be good. Yet intuitively we do seem to know what is wrong in any given situation. This is probably a hangover from the Sermon on the Mount, but is it one on the plus side for God? The Ten Commandments work well for the common good, but to consider them divinely inspired seems poppycock to me. As Erik von Danniken suggests, they could equally well have come from the pilot of some interstellar spaceship who wanted an orderly planet on which to refuel. The fact that these visits are remarkably infrequent lends substance to the theory, since we haven't exactly obeyed the rules. In the past three thousand years a spaceship would need incredibly accurate timing to land in an era of peace.

If the decline of traditional religion presents us with a meaningless world, that's too bad, but not hopeless. Ernest Becker says that in our bid for immortality we have "to fashion something—an object, or ourselves—and drop it into the confusion." I'm not much good at fashioning objects, so I concentrate on myself. Narcissism helps, says Mr. Becker. It is more than mere self-centeredness, or conceit; it is a form of self-preservation.

Occasionally I am asked how I occupy my time. The questioners are always activists who view my non-working as a personal affront, and somehow immoral to boot. They need help. Their usual solution on retirement is to join all kinds of boards and committees where they end up working as hard as before. This is not the answer. We must be kind to each other, but these people are motivated more by a need to keep themselves busy, than by the worth of the project at hand. They are not getting to the heart of the matter—a philosophic calm at the center. Beau Brummel used to say that he liked to have the morning well-aired before he got up. I agree. There's no point rushing at a day of leisure. One should shave and dress before breakfast, however, as if going somewhere. Very important for morale. A wrapper or dressing gown is permissible only on Sundays. I don't mean to sound severe; it's a good way to keep track of time. After breakfast I pick up the paper and mail in the village. Both of these could be delivered, but you need something to get you out of the house. The morning being well-advanced by then, I usually have a coffee break at Dodson's boatyard. The captious sometimes raise the question of a break between what and what, but I find you have to rise above such things.

I putter a good deal on my boat. The prime qualification for real puttering is ineptitude and this is my strong suit. Although puttering should never be measured, the following must have taken several days to complete. I wanted to put a hook on the door of the head, the idea being to keep the door ajar and not swinging when we were underway. After careful selection of a hook and an eye-screw (brass or chrome? large or small?), and after going back home for an awl, I set to work making a hole on the teak door for the eye-screw just above the lock. It was a nice deep hole into which the screw turned easily. The hook part followed with more awl work on the door frame. When in place, the hook fitted into the eye-screw, not quite in line, but enough to keep the door ajar. I had a beer and gazed at my work with pride. Working with one's hands does give satisfaction. Contemplation, however, revealed a flaw. When unhooked, the door couldn't be closed since the eye-screw protruded from the edge of the door and hit the door frame—this was not at all in keeping with a tight ship. There was nothing to do but remove the fitting completely. I sat down to finish my beer and wrote out a list of additional materials needed. Plastic wood was needed to fill the holes, also sandpaper, and a touch of stain to match the teak. Pleasurable work, to be sure, but all just to get back to square one. Fortunately, when one putters, one putters alone, so shortcomings go unnoticed. They are not at all in the same category as stocking the boat with cold cereal and having only lump sugar.

Some people go in for naps in the afternoon. I consider

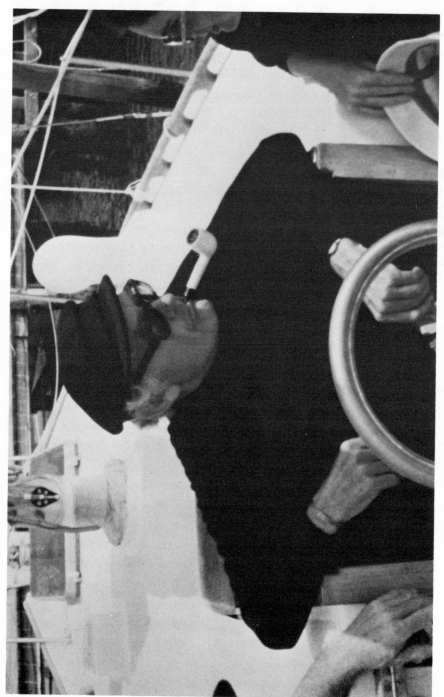

As a mariner with daughter Sylvia (who isn't one either)

this immoral, unless you are napping with someone. Generally it means one has had too many drinks before lunch. The afternoon is a time for projects. If you live in the country and also have a boat, there is always a certain amount of maintenance to be done—the septic tank may be overflowing or the jib boom may have fallen off. But these inconveniences are not what I mean. I've always felt that if you want a job done well, get somebody else to do it. What I have in mind are more creative projects—*divertissements* as the French say.

One of these was a temple I built at the end of a vista in the woods—it was a pure "folly" in the great tradition. The vista was about a quarter of a mile long, so the temple didn't have to be very substantial, just the silhouette of one. In fact the whole thing was only a three-quarter-inch-thick piece of plywood—a flight of painted steps and three columns with a rounded dome on top of a pediment, shaded on one side to give depth. When finished, it looked a bit like the old Squibb trademark, which was too bad, but it was impressive—some sixteen feet high to the top of the dome. The supporting frame was hinged so that it could be lowered in winter. Unfortunately, the lowering in the fall was a bit precipitous, owing to the weight of the dome. The plywood now serves to contain a compost heap, but for a few brief shining moments the temple was a thing of beauty—classic white against the green of the cedars. Three solid stumps still remain in the field like Palmyra in the desert.

My friend Walpole said he had a thousand ways of amusing himself. My *divertissements* also cover a wide range, and happily, most of them cost nothing. Making a walking stick can be a pleasant undertaking. First you have to select the proper branch lying about in the woods. This could take quite a time. Next you peel the bark. Then you affix a ball of plastic wood to the handle end, squeeze

The largest Max Ernst in existence? (signed "G a M"—Gus after Max)

it into the shape of your grip, sandpaper the whole, and stain it. Very satisfactory.

Sometimes I paint. Having no talent, painting is rather a makeshift arrangement with me. I have found, however, that by taking masking tape and notching the inside edge, you can lay it out on the canvas to form a perfect arc, against which you can slosh your color. Removing the tape, the effect is a fine bold line. Using this method and a ruler, I copied a little-known painting by Max Ernst called "Fighting Fish" from an illustration in a book on German expressionists. I wanted a large painting (four feet by six feet), so for every eighth of an inch in the book, I made an inch on my canvas. The result is the largest Max Ernst in existence and really quite spectacular. It even has uxorial approval—for the barn. Another painting, also about four feet by six feet, is Rousseau's "The Dream," which was measured similarly from a double page spread in a 1973 issue of *Life*. The head of the body in Rousseau's painting I found repulsive, so I substituted a head cut out of *Penthouse* magazine, which has a far more esoteric appearance on the couch in the jungle than the original. Collage we call it in the trade. It hangs over a bar in Nassau.

Then there is drama. Sometimes in the morning my granddaughter and I run through a playlet involving the window shade in my dressing room. The original script follows—

SHE: *"And the Lord said wot?"*
ME: *"Let there be light."*
SHE: *"And there was light!"*

(The child lets the shade rise slowly, and as daylight floods room, the clapping grows in volume.) Some might dismiss this scene as an advanced case of senility, but after all, the secret of perpetual youth is a firm grip on immaturity.

Punctuating the afternoon's endeavor whatever it may be, there should be tea. I know tea drinking lays one open to the charge of Anglophilia, but it's high time we forgot the Boston Tea Party. Civilized people, who have given leisure some thought, seem to have known that there is a weak point during the day that needs filling between 4:30 and 5:30 P.M. The actual libation itself is not much, although Lapsang Souchong is preferable to Orange Pekoe, but one can make as much or as little of it as required— rolled watercress sandwiches on silver plates or toast and Dundee marmalade. Following tea, I bathe at some length and put on fresh linen. If you think of the grand old days of leisure when its practitioners sometimes changed their clothes as much as four or five times a day, a tub and a clean shirt are a most pathetic link to the glorious, excessive past.

About 6:00 P.M. each day, an odd thing happens—I touch base with reality twice in rapid succession. The first contact is a cold shower after the hot tub, a habit so inbred in us at school that anyone who doesn't go in for this form of masochism strikes me as hopelessly effete. The second is the TV evening news. It's a sad commentary, but I have come to the conclusion that one needs to know what the world has been up to during the day. Maybe it's just a question of like calling to like. I sense bad attitude in all good reporters.

Sen. Fulbright points out that "there are two Americas. One is the America of Lincoln and Adlai Stevenson; the other is the America of Teddy Roosevelt and the modern superpatriots." Most media representatives belong to the first category and thereby bring down on themselves vilification by the second. We have had too much of the latter in recent years. Take for example the comment on Saigon's troops by an American helicopter pilot—"Those guys are sharp. I really enjoyed working for a guy I had on the ground. He told us the sites of the antiaircraft positions and the best approach . . . It was beautiful." Shades of Mussolini's son bombing the Ethiopians, who opened up like a rose.

Perhaps the apotheosis of the American Dream is the leadership crisis we have experienced with Watergate. A ruthless competitor who had reached the top was brought down by the other America. How dissimilar was he from many a corporate chairman? And his board of directors— the National Security Council, what about them? You can't lay the blame on any one man. The chairman takes action with his chums. Is it possible that Marx was right and that we need wars to keep industry going? I never used to think so, but I now live in an area where the biggest employer is Electric Boat, which grinds out bigger and better submarines and has been doing so for years. Recently there was a terrible furor about the Trident submarine program. If it were eliminated, tens of thousands would be out of work. Impossible. We do a lot of tut-tutting about the military-industrial complex, but it still runs on uncurtailed. My own solution might be considered radical, but I think we have to eliminate the National Security Council. I don't mean murder. They should be put to sleep with those bullets they use to subdue wild animals in the jungle. When they woke up they would find themselves in some rest camp like Silver Hill. Each one of them would be given a World Atlas and as many toy soldiers, tanks, guns, airplanes, and ships from Schwartz as he felt he needed. Every morning at the crack of dawn they would brief the chairman and in the afternoon there would be war games. At the end of the year the chairman would give out prizes. They would be well-fed, everybody could have his batman or valet, and nobody would be hurt unless he tried to escape. If some other countries would do the same I'm sure we would all get on splendidly.

A young person today has to face this basic problem. Is

he or she going to go along with the system or try to change it? It's no good just saying that we and our fathers before us made a hash of it. If that's all they do, their children will say the same—if there are any of them around. The difficulty is that the change has to come from within in a lot of people. Herbert Marcuse believes that there is a marked increase in the number of human beings "who are overcoming the aggressive, competitive values . . . who know they can live in peace without endless self-propelling productivity." I doubt if the Sunday football crowds singing the "Star-Spangled Banner" would go along with this concept. I don't believe they would go as far as the Kent State mother who said that "if anyone walks around a city like Kent with long hair, dirty clothes and barefoot, they deserve to be shot." The counterculture of the sixties questioned the essential rightness, sanity and viability of the urban industrial way of life. It created what Jean-François Revel calls "that all-enveloping and erratic sedition" with which governments cannot cope. Most of the sandal-makers and their ilk have now gone underground and joined the system, at least temporarily. This, I think, is too bad for the state of the nation and the world. It could be catastrophic.

On the other hardy perennials—death, God and the infinite—I am inclined to agree with Freud when he says, "the moment one inquires about the sense or value of life, one is sick." I've never heard that Freud was a jokester, so he undoubtedly meant it. There is a sign in the howdah of a Disneyland elephant which reads, "Please remain seated until your elephant comes to a full stop." If we are to avoid Freud's comdemnation of being sick, we should probably adopt this as our motto. Obviously, according to Freud, we are not meant to be serious. I must admit that, although the lower depths appeal to many, I have always been a surface man myself. It makes for better sleep.

In the course of growing up I've found it enjoyable, if not profitable, to pattern my life on some hero or mini-hero. You don't have to stick with him or her; in fact, you can change the type whenever it suits you. My first was D'Artagnan in *The Three Musketeers*. This was about the time I was demoted for swordplay in the Knickerbocker Greys. I think at boarding school I patterned myself in part on *Tom Brown's Schooldays* and in part on *Stalky and Co*. Next was Parsifal, the guileless fool, who blended imperceptibly into Fred Astaire, followed by Cary Grant. Somewhere along the line some figure such as J. P. Morgan should have materialized, but he didn't. Instead it was Bertie Wooster and the Drones Club. As a would-be country squire, I am now working up to Sir Roger de Coverley, the eighteenth-century character depicted in *The Spectator*. According to Addison and Steele he was a "man of many parts." He never did anything very well, but he did a lot of different things. In any given field there will always be somebody better than you, and let's hope it gives him other pleasure. Sir Roger suits me fine. The only drawback is that as a model in this day and age, he happens to be rather expensive. He lived well. A sadhu would be much cheaper, but then I can't very well walk up and down North Main Street in Stonington with a begging bowl and a loincloth. In the first place, if not immediately arrested, I would probably starve to death—and secondly, I've become more persnickety in my menus. My children, too, would be embarrassed. I can't see them pointing with pride and saying, "There's Father under his Bo tree."

Nevertheless the East has its fascination. I would be the first to say that I'm a little weak on psychic growth, but I recognize there is a validity in the concept. Sad to say, we in the West are as inept in its practices as any aborigine facing a computer. I'm not good at computers either, but there's something tangible about a computer that could conceivably be grasped, whereas it's hard to get hold of anything in the East. Breathing properly is all very well; we can learn that quite easily and it's understandable. More oxygen in the blood. But from that to merging with the infinite is a long step for mankind. Yet we need the East, because our own people have let us down. It is, in fact, surprising that anything we now call truth emerged from the thinkers of the Christian era, haunted as they were by the Pauline myths of original sin, eternal damnation and the need for personal salvation. As Lin Yutang says, "You can't make a man a Christian unless you first make him believe that he is a sinner."

Leaving aside original sin, which has never grabbed me, I have indulged in the seven deadly ones, but never all of them at once. Pride, lust, and sloth are more my bag than the others. It doesn't seem to me, however, that God has any business mucking about in such humble, temporal matters. Take suicide, for example. The idea that a suicide warrants eternal damnation is downright sadistic. Any poor devil who is so desperate that he wants to do himself in shouldn't have to worry about this little extra burden. And yet for the gift of life, the Christian is meant to be grateful forever. Merit accrues to those who fight the longest, even though terminally ill. He or she never gave in— blind, incontinent, and dumb—but still alive, by God. Crap! There should be lethal shots kept in doctors' offices with a system of keys such as they have on submarines for firing nuclear missiles. It would take at least two keys to open the drawer where it is kept. One would be permanently yours, given to you when you came of age. My dog, Buster, had such a shot. He was in my arms at the time and I asked the vet how long it would take. He said he was already dead. That kind of thing is essential. Who wants the kind of illness for which friends and relations go around afterwards saying, "Oh yes, it was a blessing that he died."

I'd rather have my vet with his needle than wait till God takes his time. In some cases I know, God hasn't gotten around for years.

Happily today, the more barbaric concepts of sin are being relegated to the Bible belts of the Western world. Christianity has taught us that man is basically bad and has dragged in God to back up its claims. An equally valid and vapid hypothesis is that man is basically good. Now it seems quite clear that God is too serious a matter to be entrusted to the Church. In an attempt to reconcile modern science with his religious faith, the Jesuit monk, Teilhard de Chardin, has written: "We have only to believe. And the more threatening and irreducible reality appears, the more firmly and desperately we must believe. Then little by little, we shall see the universal horror unbend, and smile upon us . . ." Maybe so. Others find it better not to think of the dilemma at all. "I accept the universe," said Margaret Fuller, to which Carlyle is said to have added, "By God, she'd better." Personally, I temporize with the idea that until we figure out what's behind the last star there will always be a case for God. But why does a presumably nice God play hide-and-seek with his constituents? We would all be better people (and isn't that the idea?) if God revealed himself now and again. One or two trips in a fiery cloud would do wonders for the moral climate. "Whirl is king, having driven out Zeus," said Aristophanes in a time much like our own. The old traditions have fallen. What are our contemporary values? Is there a metaphysician in the house?

Let's face it—the last big problem we have to circumvent is death, and that's not easy. Death is an unpleasant arrangement. Aside from the worry and physical discomfort, it is a nasty blow to the ego. Certainly the greatest tragedy in my life will be my own demise. The thought of personal extinction goes against the grain. I cannot accept the idea

Today

that I am merely an atom in a sea of mud or, as Carl Sagan says, a temporary repository for nucleic acid. There must be more to it all than that. Most religions try to solve the problem with a lot of pablum about the afterlife, but "religion," says Fred Hoyle, the astronomer, "is but a desperate attempt to find an escape from the truly dreadful situation in which we find ourselves . . . While our intelligences are powerful enough to penetrate deeply into the evolution of this incredible universe, we still have not the smallest clue to our own fate." God may not play dice with the world, but somebody sure is stacking the cards.

Astronomers are now saying that planets around a star are a fairly common occurrence and that in our galaxy alone there are 600 million planets capable of supporting life as we know it. That's quite a lot of lebensraum. It would be nice to think that our souls progress from planet to planet, and that those of our dogs and cats do the same. Biologists, however, believe that the universe is teeming with life, in which case the present occupants of any given planet would probably look askance at what would amount to a daily infiltration of dogs, cats and foreigners. A group of wan souls from Earth, somewhat shaken by their recent experiences, would come in at the bottom of the pecking order. You might well end up as a potboy or tweenie and never see the light of Alpha Centauri except on your Sundays off.

One can go off the deep end thinking about space. For those who need it, there may be a prime mover out there, obviously rather a shy type hiding in some black hole. If so, we must be staunch enough to realize that the press of galactic business is such as to preclude any interest in us as individuals. If there is someone in charge, he, she or it has too many juggling balls in the air to give us the time of day.

Where does that leave my friend, the dweller within my

body? We can't rule him out entirely. He is a pretty tough nut; also he may have influence. Just the same, I think he's headed for trouble. Not to be too egocentric, how is he going to manage without my physical presence? We are used to each other; we enjoy the same things. The games with me and my friends will be over, as the Emperor Hadrian said in bidding farewell to his soul. I know mine won't like it alone when he leaves for the pale, cold regions (I'm sure he would hate a black hole), and if he turns up on earth again, possibly next time as a toad, I know he won't warm to that. He has enjoyed a favored life with me, and should he get anything less in the future, he is going to feel poorly used. Since his next go-round—whatever it is—presumably will be my fault, the only decent thing to do is to indulge him now as much as I can, in case he has to pay. Not a worthy project perhaps, but then when you get right down to it, who is making the rules?